JOSEPH
UNDERSTANDING GOD'S PURPOSE

Also available in the Studies in Faithful Living Series

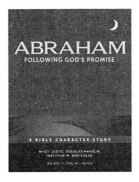

Abraham: Following God's Promise

Jacob: Discerning God's Presence

Mary: Devoted to God's Plan

For updates on this series, visit LexhamPress.com/SFL

JOSEPH

UNDERSTANDING GOD'S PURPOSE

Studies in Faithful Living

Derek R. Brown
Miles Custis
Douglas Mangum
Matthew M. Whitehead

Editor

Michael R. Grigoni

LEXHAM PRESS

Joseph: Understanding God's Purpose
Studies in Faithful Living

Copyright 2014 Lexham Press

Logos Bible Software, 1313 Commercial St., Bellingham, WA 98225
LexhamPress.com

ISBN 978-1-57-799578-4

Assistant Editors: Rebecca Brant, Lynnea Fraser, Elizabeth Vince
Cover Design: Jim LePage
Typesetting: ProjectLuz.com

TABLE OF CONTENTS

INTRODUCTION

At the beginning of Joseph's story, his life seems ideal. He is his father's favored son. His dreams seem to point to his future greatness. However, Joseph's life quickly turns tragic. Jealous of their brother's favored position and angered at his dreams of ruling over them, Joseph's brothers cast him into a pit and sell him as a slave to a passing caravan. They bring back only his bloodied robe and let their father, Jacob, conclude the worst. From this point forward, Joseph's life takes many turns. He suffers false accusations and imprisonment before being promoted to a position of power in Egypt. Through it all, Joseph remains faithful to God, and God never abandons him. Joseph's story teaches us a profound lesson: No matter our circumstances or others' actions, God will accomplish his purpose.

Looking at the "steps" that make up the lives of people like Joseph is one way to engage with the story of the Bible. This is the approach taken by the *Studies in Faithful Living* series. In this volume, we examine the life of a man who remained faithful to God despite injustice and betrayal, drawing out the lessons his faithful responses provide for us. We also see how God works behind the scenes to accomplish his greater purpose. Studying the Bible in this way teaches us to model the exceptional characters of Scripture and grow in our efforts to imitate Christ. In doing so, we enter deeper into the story the Bible narrates for us: God's redemption of creation—a story that continues in the lives of all who respond to him today.

We begin in Chapter 1 with Joseph's fall from favor as his brothers jealously sell him to passing slave traders. In Chapter 2, we see how Joseph resisted temptation and literally fled from sin. Chapter 3 shows Joseph remaining faithful in spite of suffering through a false imprisonment.

In Chapter 4, Joseph's perseverance pays off as he is promoted to a position of power in Egypt. The story shifts to Joseph's brothers in Chapter 5, portraying the guilt and shame they continued to feel years after they sold their brother. In Chapter 6, we see how Joseph chose not to take vengeance on his brothers, but to test them to see if they had changed. Chapter 7 depicts the emotional reunion between Joseph and his family, along with Joseph's recognition that God had used the many trials of his life to accomplish his greater purpose. Finally, in Chapter 8, we see Joseph forgive his brothers after his father's death.

To help you dig deeper into these biblical accounts, we've arranged each chapter into five sections. In *Setting the Stage*, we introduce the theme of the chapter and the significant literary, historical, and cultural details of the story at hand. *A Closer Look* illuminates the narrative by walking you through the story itself. *Throughout the Bible* connects the Old and New Testaments and shows how the biblical authors have understood the story under consideration at various points in biblical history. *Beyond the Bible* accomplishes a similar task by exploring the story within various historical contexts. This leads to the *Application*, where we discuss the relevance of Joseph's experiences for our lives today. Application and reflection questions conclude each chapter to help you contemplate and internalize what you've learned.

In Joseph's story, we see God accomplishing his purpose despite the intention of others. Joseph endured suffering for many years: His brothers wanted to be rid of him. His refusal to sin with Potiphar's wife resulted in his false imprisonment. When a fellow prisoner could provide Joseph a chance for freedom, Joseph was forgotten for two more years. Yet through it all, God was working to accomplish his purpose. At the end of his story, Joseph recognized God's greater purpose for his life. He told his brothers, "you planned evil against me, but God planned it for good, in order to do this—to keep many people alive—as it is today" (Gen 50:20). May this study encourage you to recognize how God's sovereign purposes are being accomplished in your life.

CHAPTER 1

FALLING FROM FAVOR

Read Genesis 37:1–36.

SETTING THE STAGE

Theme. Life is filled with highs and lows, straights and crossroads. We rarely have a clear picture of how our day-to-day experiences string together to make up our life as a whole. And yet we know that God weaves his grand plan with the threads of our individual stories. It's usually only through hindsight that we can see how he's been at work all along.

The story of Joseph is such a tale—one with tatters and frayed ends that may appear to be a life unraveling. But as time passed and God orchestrated his circumstances, Joseph could say that God had, indeed, woven a masterpiece of good. Joseph's story opens with a tragic betrayal by his brothers. Yet in spite of such treachery, Joseph would come to recognize the sovereign providence of God (Gen 50:20). And we can have the same confidence that God is at work in every situation we face (Rom 8:28).

Literary Context. Joseph's story begins in Genesis 37 and continues to the end of the book (chapter 50), making it the longest complete narrative in Genesis. Not only does it tell the story of Joseph's rise from the mire of a Canaanite pit to the right hand of Pharaoh, it help us understand why God's people are suddenly enslaved in Egypt when we reach the first chapters of Exodus.

> **Quick Bit:** Genesis 37 opens with "the generations (*toledoth*) of Jacob" (Gen 37:2a). Throughout Genesis, the Hebrew word *toledoth* is

used to mark major sections or introduce genealogies. In Genesis 2:4 "the *toledoth* of the heavens and the earth" introduces the account of Adam and Eve in the garden of Eden. In Genesis 6:9 it introduces the story of Noah. The *toledoth* of Terah introduces the story of his son Abraham (Gen 11:27). The phrase is used throughout Genesis (see Gen 5:1; 10:1, 32; 11:10; 25:12, 19).

Joseph's story revolves around the ongoing rivalry between Joseph and his 10 brothers, a hatred born of their father's favoritism. To understand how this family dynamic developed, we have to go back to the story of Jacob and his wives. We know from Genesis 29–30 that Jacob loved Rachel and chose her as his wife. For seven years he served her father, Laban, to earn the right to marry her. At the wedding, however, Laban tricked Jacob into marrying his older daughter, Leah. To marry Rachel, Jacob had to work for another seven years and pay a second bride price. Even though his marriage to Leah was fruitful, Jacob loved Rachel more. She was the woman he desired from the moment they met (see Gen 29:30).

Leah bore Jacob six sons (Reuben, Simeon, Levi, Judah, Issachar, and Zebulun); he had two more sons with Leah's servant, Zilpah (Gad and Asher). Jacob also had two sons with Rachel's servant, Bilhah (Dan and Naphtali). All this time, Rachel was unable to conceive. Eventually, Rachel gave birth to Joseph (Gen 30:22–23). Later, she died while giving birth to their second son, Benjamin (Gen 35:16-20).

Joseph was his father's favorite because he was Rachel's firstborn son. Her untimely death likely contributed to Jacob's continued preference for Joseph, but this partiality demoralized the other brothers. In sharing his dreams with them, Joseph only amplified their anger. Eventually, their simmering envy and bitterness boiled over, and they rid themselves of their irritation: They sold Joseph to passing slave traders bound for Egypt (Gen 37:27-28).

Historical & Cultural Background. The slave trade was a thriving industry in the ancient world. Dothan, where Joseph's brothers pastured their flock, was situated along the major caravan route running from Gilead to Egypt. Caravans carried goods such as spices, myrrh, and balm from southern Arabia to Egypt.[1] They also transported slaves from

Syria and Canaan. Egyptian documents show that the sale of such slaves was common.²

Joseph's brothers sold him for 20 shekels of silver, the typical price for slaves of Joseph's age (see Lev 27:5) and a little more than double what a shepherd earned in a year. (A hired shepherd could expect to make about eight shekels a year.³) After they arrived in Egypt, the traders sold Joseph again, this time to Potiphar, an Egyptian official. Wealthy officials like Potiphar bought slaves for household chores and fieldwork—barely a step up from the pit for Jacob's favorite son.

The adolescent Joseph must have felt frightened and confused by this degrading turn of events. As he tumbled from a comfortable perch as his father's favorite child into the darkness of the pit and the indignity of a foreign slave market, he must have doubted his bright visions of the future. But God was accomplishing his purpose through these difficult circumstances, and he would bless Joseph: The beloved son turned slave would gain Potiphar's trust and rise to a position of authority within his house (Gen 39:2-6).

A CLOSER LOOK

Joseph, the favored son of Jacob, was young and boisterous. At age 17, he pastured the flock with his older brothers and then tattled on them to their father (Gen 37:2). He wore the special robe his father gave him and did not seem to notice that his brothers hated him. When he shared his lofty dreams, he added fuel to the fire of their jealousy.

> **Quick Bit:** Dreams were taken seriously in the ancient world. People believed they were messages from the gods, containing omens and symbols that revealed the future.

Joseph was a dreamer—literally. He experienced extremely vivid, meaningful visions. In Genesis 37:5-11, Joseph tells his family about two of his dreams, both of which strain his tenuous relationship with his brothers.

In the first dream, Joseph binds sheaves of grain with his brothers. His sheaf stands tall, while his brothers' bundles gather around and bow before his (Gen 37:7). There's no mystery about the meaning of this dream, and the brothers fire back, "Will you really rule over us?" The narrative emphasizes their response: the brothers "hated him even more on account of his dream and because of his words" (Gen 37:8).

But Joseph doesn't hesitate to tell them about his second dream, sharing this one with his father as well. This time the sun, moon, and eleven stars cluster around him to bow down (Gen 37:9). Jacob echoes his sons (Gen 37:10). Would *he*—the patriarch and head of the household—also bow down to Joseph? Readers are left to wonder whether the dreams' implications are apparent to everyone but the dreamer.

> **Quick Bit:** The question of Joseph's motivation reflects the ambiguity inherent in reading a narrative. We can view Joseph's character sympathetically or critically. We can give him the benefit of the doubt—he is naïve and foolish—or we can assume the worst—he is calculating and arrogant. Narrators give us clues, but sometimes we have to be content with ambiguity.

The sparse details in the narrative leave Joseph's motive open to interpretation. Yet we cannot help but wonder *why* Joseph shared the dreams. Was he trying to anger his brothers? This seems unlikely since he had no fear when leaving his father's protection to check on them in Dothan (Gen 37:17-20). If he intended to provoke them, he should have expected retaliation. Was he calculating and ambitious, scheming his way into authority over his brothers? This also seems unlikely for the same reason. A cunning and crafty Joseph would have already noted his brothers' anger and suspected their potential for foul play. He would not have wandered into their camp carefree.

Why then, did the teenager essentially taunt his family? We cannot be sure, but our own experience can lend insight. Joseph had grown up as the apple of his father's eye. His enjoyed a privileged childhood, and such experience often blinds us to the evils in the world—specifically to evils directed at us. Joseph must have thought, "How could anyone hate *me*?"

But when the opportunity arose, the brothers seized the moment to eliminate their upstart rival. Both father and son *must* have been blind to the brothers' hatred, because Jacob casually sent Joseph out to check on them in Shechem, some 50 miles north of Jacob's camp at Hebron (Gen 37:12-14).

Once there, Joseph learned that his brothers had moved further north to Dothan on the southern edge of the plain of Jezreel, another 15 miles away (Gen 37:15–17).

The narrative reveals that the brothers saw Joseph coming "from a distance" and made plans to kill him (Gen 37:18–20). Perhaps Joseph's coat of many colors made him recognizable from afar. Their desire to keep his dreams from coming true fueled their conspiracy (Gen 37:20). In a scene of dramatic irony, the brothers' actions to thwart their little brother set in motion the very events that would lead to Joseph's rise to power and the ultimate fulfillment of his visions.

Before Joseph fell into their hands, his oldest brother, Reuben, came to his rescue by persuading the others to throw him in a nearby pit instead of killing him (Gen 37:21). Reuben's actions add another layer of irony: As the eldest of Jacob's sons, Reuben would have expected to hold a place of prominence among the brothers—an expectation threatened by the message of Joseph's dreams. But Reuben had wronged Jacob in the past and was likely eager to curry his father's favor.

After the death of Rachel (Jacob's favorite wife), Reuben violated his father's trust by sleeping with Bilhah, the concubine who bore sons for Jacob on Rachel's behalf (Gen 35:22). Reuben may have acted in presumption of his succession, or in a ploy to ensure that his own mother, Leah, would be the primary matriarch of the clan, rather than Bilhah.[4] In either case, his brothers' murderous intentions gave Reuben the chance to get back into Jacob's good graces. Convincing the brothers to throw Joseph in a pit, he planned to sneak back, rescue Joseph, and take him home to Jacob (Gen 37:22).

> **Quick Bit:** The pit was a cistern dug into rock or clay to collect water during rainy seasons (Gen 37:24). Often bottle shaped with covered openings, cisterns could also serve as hiding places (1 Sam 13:6) and temporary prisons (Jer 38:6). In the arid climate of Israel, cisterns were symbols of wealth and prosperity (Deut 6:11; 2 Kgs 18:31).

Stripped of his special robe, Joseph must have been stunned to find himself at the bottom of a well while the conspirators sat down for dinner (Gen 37:23–25). When a caravan of Ishmaelite traders appeared on the horizon, it was Judah's idea to sell Joseph—and convincing his brothers was easy. They may as well make money off their bothersome brother instead of having his blood on their hands. Judah appealed to what little conscience the brothers may have had: "He *is* our brother, our own flesh" (Gen 37:26–27).

Reuben, who had left the camp for a while, returned to find the pit empty (Gen 37:29). Distraught—likely over his lost opportunity to regain his father's favor—he tore his clothes in mourning (Gen 37:19–30). The brothers did not tell Reuben what had really happened, leaving him to believe that they killed Joseph while he was gone. After dipping Joseph's coat in the blood of a slaughtered goat, the brothers sent the robe to Jacob with a message: "We found this; please examine it. Is it the robe of your son or not?" (Gen 37:32). As the brothers knew he would, Jacob drew his own heart-wrenching conclusion: A fierce animal had torn Joseph to pieces (Gen 37:33). Jacob intended to mourn until he died (Gen 37:35). If Reuben could have, he likely would have snatched the chance to save his father from this fate by telling him the truth. But the brothers' dreadful secret was safe. And they didn't even have to lie.

While Jacob wept in Canaan, Joseph arrived at the Egyptian slave market, where a powerful officer of Pharaoh bought him (Gen 37:36). Joseph's life had been turned upside down, and though we do not hear directly from him in the text, we can imagine the darkness and despair he must feel. What possible purpose could this sorrow and suffering serve? He could not imagine what God was doing, and it would be many years before he would see the big picture.

THROUGHOUT THE BIBLE

Favoritism fueled the fire of contention between Joseph and his brothers. Jacob loved Joseph best (Gen 37:3), and the rest of the clan resented it. Jacob believed Joseph's word over his other sons (Gen 37:2), tolerated his dreams of grandeur, and gave only a soft rebuke when Joseph pushed against his fatherly authority (Gen 37:10).

The Bible has much to say about the pitfalls of partiality. In the ot, favoritism is usually associated with injustice and bribery. The law of Moses warns against showing partiality when rendering a verdict: "You shall not do injustice in judgment; you shall not show partiality to the powerless; you shall not give preference to the powerful; you shall judge your fellow citizen with justice" (Lev 19:15). Deuteronomy 1:17 repeats this command, "You must not be partial in judging: hear out the small and the great alike; you shall not be intimidated by anyone, for the judgment is God's."

As in the OT, the NT describes God as fair and just, "For there is no partiality with God" (Rom 2:11; see also Acts 10:34; Gal 2:6; Eph 6:9). Surprisingly, Jesus' opponents described him as impartial: "So they sent their disciples to him, along with the Herodians, saying, 'Teacher, we know that you are sincere, and teach the way of God in accordance with truth, and show deference to no one; for you do not regard people with partiality' " (Matt 22:16 NRSV).

But it's James who condemns partiality most harshly. As a leader in the early church, James witnessed Christians showing preference for wealthy members over poor ones (Jas 2:1-13). In his letter, James asks his audience a rhetorical question: "My brothers and sisters, do you with your acts of favoritism really believe in our glorious Lord Jesus Christ?" (Jas 2:1 NRSV). He said those who played favorites were like evil judges, and he condemned them for it: "But if you show partiality, you commit sin, and thus are convicted by the law as transgressors" (Jas 2:9; also 2:4). His solution to the problem of partiality was simple. He issued the command: "Carry out the royal law according to the scripture, 'You shall love your neighbor as yourself'" (Jas 2:8; see Lev 19:18).

In this statement James articulates Jesus' ethic (compare Jas 2:8 with Mark 12:31; John 13:34). Yet during Jesus' earthly life, James and the rest of Jesus' brothers opposed his ministry (Mark 3:21, 31; John 7:1-5), just as Joseph's brothers opposed him. Eventually, however, James came full circle (as did Joseph's brothers) and instructed fellow Christians to live and act as Jesus did. He went so far as to describe "wisdom from above" as "without a trace of partiality" (Jas 3:17).

It's clear in both Testaments that any expression of favoritism is wrong and likely to produce disastrous consequences. Jacob's disproportionate love for Joseph alienated him from his brothers and eventually led to his enslavement. Jacob's partiality also led to his greatest heartache—the loss of his son.

BEYOND THE BIBLE

Joseph's life parallels the life of Jesus in many ways. Both men were loved by their fathers but despised by their brothers. Both received promises of future greatness, were betrayed for silver, and experienced exile in Egypt.

These similarities led some Christians to interpret Joseph's story typologically. This method of interpretation considers OT people and events to prefigure people and events in the NT.[5] Typology often had a messianic focus and viewed OT characters as prefiguring Christ and the events of his ministry. For example, the sacrifice of Isaac was considered a "type" that found its ultimate significance in Jesus' death and resurrection.

> **Quick Bit:** Ambrose (ca. AD 333–397), one of the church fathers, ministered as the bishop of Milan. He gained a reputation as an influential theologian and teacher. He is perhaps best known as the instructor of the theologian Augustine.

Ambrose of Milan, an early church father who used typology, considered Joseph to prefigure Jesus. He understood Joseph's first dream (Gen 37:5–8) as a foreshadowing of Christ's resurrection: "Now in this the resurrection of the Lord Jesus that was to come was revealed. When they saw him at Jerusalem, the eleven disciples and all the saints bowed down; when they rise, they will bow down bearing the fruits of their good works."[6] When Jacob sent Joseph to get a report about his brothers in Shechem (Gen 37:12–14), Ambrose discerned another foreshadowing: "And so Jacob, in sending his son to his brothers to see if it was well with the sheep, foresaw the mysteries of the incarnation that was to come."[7] Ambrose even saw a reference to Jesus' death on the cross in the Joseph story (Gen 37:23):

> Accordingly, even at that time, the cross that was to come was prefigured in sign; and at the same time that he was stripped of his tunic, that is, of the flesh he took on, he was stripped of the handsome diversity of colors that represented the virtues. Therefore his tunic, that is, his flesh, was stained with blood, but not his divinity; and

his enemies were able to take from him his covering of flesh but not his immortal life.[8]

In their zeal for Christ, biblical interpreters were compelled to find him throughout the OT, and typology enabled them to do so. They saw him at work, even in the painful moments of Joseph's story, bringing about our eventual redemption through Christ.

Although typological interpretations of Scripture can sometimes produce fanciful and questionable conclusions, Ambrose's use of this method emphasizes an important insight: God was with Joseph, even in his darkest hour, to work out his plan of redemption. Although Joseph didn't know where the terrible events of Genesis 37 would lead, God was moving behind the scenes to bring about the salvation of his people.

APPLICATION

Joseph's story illustrates how disaster can capsize a man's life. The narrative introduces Joseph as the favorite son, destined for greatness, but it rapidly shifts to a tale of vengeance, suffering, and enslavement. The chapter ends with great suspense: Will God deliver Joseph from his hopeless predicament? Will his brothers ever answer for their horrible actions?

In many ways the cliffhanger at the end of Genesis 37 resembles the uncertain times in our own lives. Like Joseph, we rarely know what happens in the next chapter of our story. Joseph certainly didn't know—and probably didn't dare imagine—that his experiences in Egypt could ever be used for good. In such times, our shortsighted vision of the future blinds us from seeing the faithfulness of God. As believers, we are called to trust him even when uncertainty and confusion prevail.

Thankfully, God's providence exceeds the scope of our comprehension. The Bible offers many accounts of individuals who chose to trust God in the face of doubt. When Jesus confronted suffering in the garden of Gethsemane, he placed his fate into God's hands: "Father, if you are willing, take away this cup from me. Nevertheless, not my will, but yours, be done" (Luke 22:42). The Apostle Paul agonized over a "thorn in the flesh" and begged God to take it away: "Three times I pleaded with the Lord about this, that it should leave me" (2 Cor 12:7–8). And he clung to God's response: "My grace is sufficient for you" (2 Cor 12:9).

When disappointment or tragedy threaten to tear us apart, the idea of God's goodness and sovereignty seems to mock us. And yet it is true— and we must believe. By his grace and in his time, we may even get to glimpse the big picture. We may stand with Joseph and say God meant it all for good.

DISCUSSION

A Closer Look

1. Reflect on the negative impact favoritism has on Joseph's family. How can you work to overcome jealousy and strife in your own relationships?

_____

_____

_____

2. Joseph might be a conceited know-it-all or an innocent victim. Have you ever failed to give someone the benefit of the doubt and thought worse of them than they deserved?

_____

_____

_____

Throughout the Bible

1. Why was Joseph Jacob's favorite son? Who seems to have taken over that role once Jacob thought Joseph was dead? Why?

_____

_____

_____

2. In what ways do we show favoritism in our relationships? How can we correct this?

_____

_____

_____

Beyond the Bible

1. What other parallels do you notice between the lives of Joseph and Jesus?

_____

_____

_____

2. How does God's continued presence with Joseph give you hope?

_____

_____

_____

Application

1. Recall a time in your life when you felt nothing good could come from your situation. How did you respond? How did God act?

_____

_____

_____

2. What stories of God's faithfulness might Joseph have recalled while he was in prison? What stories in Scripture can we draw on when we need help looking beyond our limited perspective?

_____

_____

_____

CHAPTER 2

SUCCESS AND SEDUCTION

Read Genesis 39:1-23.

SETTING THE STAGE

Theme. We are all susceptible to temptations in life. Some are like old friends we run into several times a year. But others seem to come out of nowhere—dangerous enticements that blindside us, giving us no chance to prepare. Jesus warned us that temptations would come (Matt 18:7). And when they do, we can either allow them to gain a foothold, or we can stand firm and resist their advance. Joseph was prepared to withstand temptation, and when it came, he not only resisted—he fled.

Joseph had found stability in Egypt as the trusted slave of Potiphar, one of Pharaoh's officials. But no sooner had he established himself than he was abruptly faced by temptation, seemingly out of nowhere. Potiphar's wife had set her sights on Joseph and determined to seduce him. He refused her, citing his allegiance to both God and Potiphar (Gen 39:8-9). But she persisted until Joseph literally ran from her, leaving his cloak behind. His faithfulness was rewarded with a prison cell. Although Joseph couldn't see it yet, God honored his integrity and acted to secure his future, orchestrating all these events for his benefit and for the good of his family.

Literary Context. Picking up from the cliffhanger at the end of Genesis 37, Joseph's narrative continues in Genesis 39. Between these chapters, Genesis 38 tells the story of Judah (Joseph's older brother) and Tamar.

While Genesis 38 may seem to have little connection to Joseph's account, its events actually play a significant role in the overarching narrative—not only that of Joseph, but also in the story that leads to the birth of Jesus.

After Joseph was sold to Potiphar, Judah left his brothers to start a family (Gen 38:1–5). Judah's firstborn son married a woman named Tamar, but Yahweh put him to death (Gen 38:6–7). Judah's second oldest son then married Tamar, but Yahweh also killed him (Gen 38:10). Seeing this, Judah instructed Tamar to live as a widow and wait until his youngest son was old enough to marry (Gen 38:11). But Judah had no intention of having his youngest son marry Tamar considering the fate of his two older sons (Gen 38:14).

Tamar later tricked Judah into sleeping with her by disguising herself as a prostitute (Gen 38:13–16). In exchange for sex, he promised her a young goat. She kept his signet, cord, and staff as a pledge. Before Judah could return to fulfill the pledge, she fled the site of their encounter (Gen 38:17–23). Tamar became pregnant and was later brought before Judah, her father-in-law, on the charge of immorality. With Judah's signet, cord, and staff, Tamar exposed his role in the affair (Gen 38:24–25). Judah—who had shirked his responsibility to Tamar—declared that she was more righteous than he (Gen 38:26).

Several similarities between the stories of Judah and Joseph link the brothers and hint at Judah's future importance. Both were separated from their brothers, although under different circumstances (Gen 38:1). Both also faced sexual temptation, but they responded differently (Gen 39:7–12; 38:15–19). Both Judah and Joseph's brothers eventually bow down to them: to Joseph at the conclusion of his story (Gen 44:14), and metaphorically to Judah as Jacob blesses him (Gen 49:8). And both stories demonstrate God's sovereign work to save his people: God used Joseph to save his family from famine, whereas Judah and Tamar's descendants became the forebears of the Savior of the world (Matt 1:3; see Chapter 8: "Throughout the Bible").

Historical & Cultural Background. In Egypt, Joseph excelled in his work for his master, Potiphar, and was eventually promoted. Joseph became "overseer of his house" (Gen 39:4 ESV). In ancient Egypt, "overseer" (Egyptian *mer-per* or i'my-r pr) was an official position. Ancient Egyptian texts describe overseers who were appointed to manage cattle or grana-ries.[1] Pharaohs also appointed overseers to royal administrative positions, supervising treasuries or temples or the royal household. Sometimes overseers were responsible for entire cities or regions (see Gen 41:34).

As overseer of Potiphar's house, Joseph most likely managed all the do-mestic activities of the estate. In blessing Joseph, God extended his blessing to Potiphar and his entire household. Joseph's stay in Egypt was already beginning to fulfill the promise God made to Abraham years be-fore: to bless all the "families of the earth" through him and his descen-dants (Gen 12:1-3).

A CLOSER LOOK

Imagine the bewildering grief you would feel arriving in a strange land as a captive. While the narrative doesn't provide all the details, we see that Joseph landed on his feet in a relatively short time. He quickly earned the respect of Potiphar, his new master. God was with Joseph, orchestrating his success (Gen 39:2-3).

Observing Joseph's exceptional work, Potiphar promoted him to the head of his household. Joseph may have been a slave, but he soon found himself in charge of the other slaves, as well as Potiphar's business af-fairs (Gen 39:4). Joseph's new position granted him great influence and responsibility—Potiphar entrusted him with everything he owned. And because of Joseph, God blessed Potiphar's household with great pros-perity (Gen 39:5-6). Yet, once again, Joseph's favor serves as a prelude to catastrophe. Despite his success and advancement, he suffers another re-versal of fortune—again, through no fault of his own.

Only 17 years old when his story opens (Gen 37:2), Joseph was undoubt-edly still a young man when Potiphar's wife made her advance—per-haps in his late teens or early twenties. And he was strikingly handsome (Gen 39:6). Potiphar's wife made it abundantly clear that she desired him, and she tried to pressure him into a sexual liaison. Not wishing to sin, Joseph refused her every attempt, maintaining his loyalty both to Potiphar and to God. His refusal shows incredible strength of character in one so young and powerless—he was, after all, still a slave. The narrative never suggests that Potiphar's wife was old or unattractive. In fact, artistic depictions of this scene often portray her as a seductive siren. Thus the story presents only Joseph's integrity and steadfast refusal.

In response to the initial advance, Joseph tried to reason with Potiphar's wife (Gen 39:7–9). He subtly appealed to her position in the household—as the master's wife, she was the only one not subject to Joseph's authority. And Potiphar was entitled to her loyalty. Joseph recognized the precariousness of the situation. Rape and adultery in the ancient Near East carried harsh penalties—usually execution for the guilty parties. And yet, Joseph also recognized that if he angered her by his continual refusal, she could seek revenge by trumping up charges against him.

Potiphar's wife would not relent (Gen 39:10). She pursued him day after day, trying to wear down his resistance. Like the proverbial "forbidden woman" (see "Throughout the Bible"), we can imagine her hounding Joseph with flattering and seductive requests (although the story records no more than her coarse command to "lie with" her). Joseph continued to rebuff her, holding fast to his integrity and his commitment to honor Potiphar and God. When she finally lost patience with Joseph, she seized him by his outer robe, demanding that he lie with her (Gen 39:11–12).

> **Quick Bit:** The Hebrew verb *shakhav* ("lie down") is one of the most common euphemisms for sexual intercourse in the OT (parallel to the English idiom "sleep with"). Potiphar's wife makes a two-word demand of Joseph: *shikhvah immi* ("lie with me!"). These demands are explicit sexual advances couched in euphemistic language.

Surprised by the aggression of his would-be seducer, Joseph pulled away, leaving his robe behind. He literally fled from her, leaving the house. For the second time, Joseph's robe will be used in a deception against him.[2]

Potiphar's wife seized the opportunity to punish Joseph for rejecting her advances. She accused him of attempted rape, presenting the robe as evidence (Gen 39:13–15). Her first accusation plays on Egyptian xenophobia and distrust of foreigners: "Look! [My husband] brought a Hebrew man to us to mock us!" (Gen 39:14). With these words, Potiphar's wife divided the household—the Egyptians on her side and Joseph, the Hebrew, and Potiphar on the other. Potiphar's wife likely feared that her husband would believe Joseph's word over hers. By involving the rest of the household, she could force his hand. Perhaps the other servants also resented the promotion of a foreigner over them. It is unlikely that Potiphar's wife could pursue Joseph so single-mindedly without giving herself away to the rest of the household. But the resentment of the others might overcome any lingering skepticism they had about the real culprit.

When Potiphar arrived, his wife spun a story that sealed Joseph's fate. Rather than provide the detail of her first accusation, she begins by accusing Joseph of mocking her (Gen 39:17). And as she cried out, she claims, Joseph fled, leaving his robe behind (Gen 39:18). This abridged version of the accusation is probably intended only to remind the reader of her initial accusation. In fact, the report of her accusation in Genesis 39:19 is even more vague: "This is what your servant did to me."

Angered by the report, Potiphar threw Joseph into prison (Gen 39:19-20). Yet this punishment indicates that Potiphar did not entirely believe his wife. Imprisonment was not the typical response to rape or attempted rape in ancient Egypt. Potiphar would have been justified in executing Joseph on the basis of his wife's accusations.[3] The narrative fails to indicate with whom Potiphar was angry. His anger may have been kindled against his wife for stirring up the household and costing him Joseph as his overseer. Uncertain of the truth of the accusation, yet unable to overlook it, Potiphar's hands were tied.

God was at work on Joseph's behalf even in this second reversal of fortune. Joseph quickly rose to a privileged position in his new environment (Gen 39:21-23). The scene ends much as it began: God is with Joseph, orchestrating his success so that his masters will entrust him with greater and greater responsibility (compare Gen 39:2-6 and 39:21-23). This change of scenery is simply part of the plan.

THROUGHOUT THE BIBLE

Readers of Scripture in the ancient world viewed Joseph's story as a model, not only of resistance in the face of temptation, but of wisdom. Books such as Proverbs, Ecclesiastes, and Job elaborate on the relationship between wisdom, action, and blessing. In particular, Proverbs 1-9 discusses the necessity of wisdom in resisting the "forbidden woman," whose temptations lead to sin and death. In certain respects, Potiphar's wife embodies this "forbidden woman" and would have been categorized as such in the ancient world.

Proverbs warns against the "forbidden woman" or "adulteress" (Prov 2:16-19), who ignores her marriage vows and pursues young men.[4] Proverbs describes the "forbidden woman" as tempting and alluring—a woman whose lips drip honey (Prov 5:3) as she flatters young men with smooth and seductive speech (Prov 7:21). She acts boldly with no regard for her husband (Prov 7:13, 19-20). She goes to great lengths to seduce, perfuming her bed and covering it with fine Egyptian linens (Prov 7:16-18).

Proverbs warns young men to keep far from her (Prov 5:8). It advises them to avoid the trap of her beauty and tempting words (Prov 6:25; 7:25). Succumbing to her temptation leads only to death and destruction (Prov 2:18-19). She might appear sweet and appealing, but she is bitter and costly in the end (Prov 5:3-14). Proverbs likens those who are seduced by the "forbidden woman" to oxen led to the slaughter and birds rushing into snares (Prov 7:21-23).

Proverbs offers advice on avoiding temptation. First, it advocates following the instructions of the father. If a young man keeps these commandments in mind, he will stay on the right path and thus avoid the adulteress (Prov 6:20-24). Second, Proverbs promotes wisdom as a shield against temptation. The book contrasts the call of wisdom (Prov 8:1-3) and the call of the "forbidden woman" (Prov 7:6-12). The wise young man holds fast to wisdom (Prov 7:4-5).

Blessings are in store for those who avoid temptation, according to Proverbs. Those who live uprightly and with integrity will prosper ("dwell in the land"; Prov 2:21-22). However, this statement—like others throughout Proverbs[5]—is not a promise. Instead, it communicates the principle that those who live wisely and righteously will find success. For Joseph, resisting the call of the adulteress did not bring blessing, not immediately. Rather, his path to success required a detour through prison.

BEYOND THE BIBLE

Genesis 39 has several parallels with the ancient Egyptian story *The Two Brothers*. Both accounts relate the temptations of righteous men, as well as the difficulties that arise from their fidelity. Both stories end with the vindication of the hero and his elevation to a position in the royal court. Each story emphasizes the personal and familial blessings that accompany the hero's integrity, as well as the active involvement of the hero's deity in his life.

> **Quick Bit:** *The Two Brothers* was written during Egypt's 19th Dynasty (ca. 1295–1186 BC) and preserved in Papyrus D'Orbiney, which dates to approximately 1225 BC. This date makes *The Two Brothers* roughly contemporaneous with the setting of the Joseph story.[6]

Of particular interest is the first part of the story and its relation to Genesis 39. *The Two Brothers* begins by introducing Anubis, the older, and Bata, the younger. Bata served Anubis and was in charge of his household (compare Gen 39:2–4). He was a man of character and moral excellence and is described in much the same way Genesis later describes Joseph: "Indeed, his young brother was an excellent man. There was none like him in the whole land, for a god's strength was in him" (compare Gen 41:38).[7]

One day Anubis accompanied Bata to the field to plant crops. When they ran low on seed, he sent him back to the house to fetch more. Upon entering the house, Bata requested the seed from Anubis' wife. What happens next closely parallels the Joseph narrative (compare Gen 39:6–7):

> Then she [spoke to] him saying: "There is [great] strength in you. I see your vigor daily." And she desired to know him as a man. She got up, took hold of him, and said to him: "Come, let us spend an hour lying together. It will be good for you. And I will make fine clothes for you."[8]

Like Joseph, Bata refused to have sex with his brother's/master's wife (compare Gen 39:8–9). He protested: "Look, you are like a mother to me; and your husband is like a father to me. He who is older than I has raised me. What is this great wrong you said to me? Do not say it to me again!"[9]

He promised to keep the matter between the two of them and returned to the field.

Fearing that Bata would tell Anubis what she'd done, Anubis' wife pretended he had beaten her. Her lie is similar to the one told by Potiphar's wife:

> When [your younger brother] came to take seed to you, he found me sitting alone. He said to me: "Come, let us spend an hour lying together; loosen your braids." So he said to me. But I would not listen to him. "Am I not your mother? Is your elder brother not like a father to you?" So I said to him. He became frightened and he beat me, so as to prevent me from telling you. Now if you let him live, I shall die! Look, when he returns, do not let him live! For I am ill from this evil design which he was about to carry out in the morning."[10]

Enraged by this news, Anubis tried—albeit unsuccessfully—to kill Bata (compare Gen 39:19-20). At this point the two stories diverge. Bata entreated his god for help, and his god intervened. Bata convinced his brother of his innocence and was vindicated his eyes; Anubis returned home and killed his wife for her betrayal. Eventually Bata became Pharaoh and, upon his death, his brother assumed his throne.

Although the stories are similar in many points, the Genesis account clearly emphasizes that God acted in every circumstance, preparing Joseph for the role that he would ultimately play in preserving his family and the nation of Israel. God was with Joseph and blessed him in Potiphar's house (Gen 39:2-6); he was also with him when the situation took a turn for the worse (Gen 39:21-23). Despite the opposition Joseph faced, God carried out his plan to position him in Pharaoh's administration. God used the direst situations in Joseph's life to bless him, his family, and the nation of Israel.

APPLICATION

When we think of temptation, we tend to think only of our personal issues and rarely give a thought to others facing such concerns. But temptation is an interpersonal issue that draws people into a tangled web and damages relationships. This was certainly the case for Joseph in Genesis 39. After he gained Potiphar's trust, he faced a temptation that threatened to ruin everything for him.

How could a vital young man flee such temptation? Joseph established boundaries and refused to cross them: his obligation to Potiphar and his obedience to God (Gen 39:8–9). Joseph knew that yielding to temptation would affect people besides Potiphar's wife and himself. He knew it would damage his relationship with God, destroy Potiphar's respect and cost him his position—even shatter Potiphar's relationship with his wife. So Joseph refused to compromise his integrity, even though his decision launched him into uncertainty all over again.

We find stories of temptation throughout the Bible. Adam and Eve are tempted to eat of the tree of knowledge of good and evil (Gen 3:1–7). Jesus teaches the disciples to pray for protection from temptation (Matt 6:13). And Paul writes to the Corinthians that God won't let us be tempted beyond our abilities since he is faithful (1 Cor 10:13). Those stories focus primarily on individuals' struggles with temptation. But what we learn from Joseph's story is that dealing with temptation has bigger ramifications: it involves other people and it involves God himself.

In many ways Joseph's response to Potiphar's wife anticipates Matthew 22:37–40, where Jesus sums up the Law and the Prophets in two commands: ""You shall love the Lord your God with all your heart and with all your soul and with all your mind" and "You shall love your neighbor as yourself." Joseph demonstrated his love for God and for his neighbor (Potiphar) by remaining faithful to his relationships with them.

DISCUSSION

A Closer Look

1. Reflect on a time when maintaining your integrity had an unexpectedly high price. How did you respond? Were you discouraged by the result or encouraged because you knew you did the right thing?

_____

_____

_____

2. Resisting temptation is never as easy as it looks in Joseph's story. What would you have done in Joseph's place?

_____

_____

_____

Throughout the Bible

1. Think of a time when you overcame temptation. Was there something specific that helped you resist it?

_____

_____

_____

2. What is your first response when confronted with temptation? What Bible verses help you deal with it?

_____

_____

_____

Beyond the Bible

1. Have you ever been wrongly accused of something? Were you able to prove your innocence? In what ways can you relate to Joseph's experience?

_____

_____

_____

2. Can you recall a time in your past that God protected you as a result of your integrity?

_____

_____

_____

Application

1. Think back to a significant temptation in your life. How were others involved in the situation—even if you didn't know it at the time?

_____

_____

_____

2. What boundaries in your life can you create to protect you from temptation? What boundaries might you be neglecting?

_____

_____

_____

CHAPTER 3

CONFINED BUT COURAGEOUS

Read Genesis 40:1–23.

SETTING THE STAGE

Theme. God's people are never promised a life free from suffering. In fact, Scripture assures us of just the opposite, and the Apostle James goes so far as to urge us to "consider it all joy" (Jas 1:2) when we go through trials. Although God speaks to us through every circumstance, we are often more likely to listen in times of defeat, loss, and pain. Of course, suffering may lead some people to turn against others and become bitter. It's not what we suffer but how we respond that determines whether our trials change us for the better.

Joseph endured many difficulties, from being sold into slavery by his brothers to being falsely accused of rape by his master's wife. One incident landed him in a pit, the other in a jail cell. But Joseph's trust in God never faltered. He believed God would remain faithful to his promises. In spite of repeated hardships, Joseph did not allow his heart to become bitter or resentful. Instead, he persevered.

Literary Context. Genesis 40 picks up the story of Joseph's troubles in Egypt. Despite his unjust imprisonment (Gen 39:19–20), Joseph became as successful in prison as he was in Potiphar's household (Gen 39:21–23; compare Gen 39:2–6). He was soon placed in charge of his fellow prisoners.

During this time, dreams and their interpretation return to the foreground of Joseph's story. In Genesis 37, he had two dreams in which his brothers and parents bowed down to him. By sharing these dreams, he infuriated his brothers, who sold him into slavery in an act of jealousy and rage. In Genesis 40, Joseph interprets the dreams of his fellow prisoners—the Pharaoh's baker and cupbearer. His interpretation of the cupbearer's dream eventually leads to an audience before Pharaoh in Genesis 41. There, Joseph interprets a disturbing dream even Pharaoh's wise men can't decipher.

Initially, Joseph's dreams lead to his enslavement (Gen 37). Now they contribute to his liberation and rise to power in Egypt (Gen 41)—but not before a crushing disappointment in Genesis 40. Upon his release, the cupbearer forgets the prisoner who reveals the true meaning of his dream. Yet, where so many others fail Joseph, God continues the patient and perfect unfolding of his plan.

Historical & Cultural Background. Joseph may have been imprisoned, but he was held in *Pharaoh's* prison and shared a cell with Pharaoh's chief cupbearer and baker. Before incurring Pharaoh's anger, these men were officials in the royal court. Although the role of chief baker does not appear in ancient Egyptian documents, it may be related to the "royal table scribe" who would have likely been responsible for Pharaoh's food.[1]

The role of cupbearer is better attested in ancient records. Not only did cupbearers serve wine to the king (or to Pharaoh in Egypt), they also carried the responsibility of protecting the king, especially from poison. Cupbearers were necessarily among the most loyal and trustworthy officials within a monarch's entourage, and they often became confidants or advisors to the king. Some even held political influence.[2] We see this in the story of Nehemiah, a cupbearer (Neh 1:11) who appears to have had a close relationship with King Artaxerxes of Persia (Neh 2:1–8).

In Joseph's story, Pharaoh became displeased with both his baker and cupbearer. The Bible does not tell us what the men did to upset him, but it's likely Pharaoh got sick after a meal and suspected one or both of them were responsible. Unlike common criminals or slaves, the king's servants were not cast into a dungeon for having displeased their master. They were confined to the custody of the captain of the guard, where they awaited Pharaoh's decision on their fate.

A CLOSER LOOK

When recounting this portion of Joseph's journey, storytellers often depict him in a dank, rat-infested prison. If we could go back in time, however, we would see that Joseph's circumstances were not nearly so dire.

Genesis 39:20 tells us that Potiphar put Joseph in "prison, the place that the king's prisoners were confined." This place, however, may have been another part of Potiphar's house.[3] In Hebrew, the phrase often translated "prison" literally means "house of confinement." Genesis 39:1 identifies Potiphar as the "captain of the guard," and Joseph's prison is said to be "in the house of the captain of the guard" (Gen 40:3 ESV). Thus we know that Joseph wasn't confined with thieves or murderers or common criminals. He was held among political prisoners—disgraced servants of the royal court.

Having incurred Pharaoh's wrath, two of those servants—the cupbearer and baker—were confined in the house of the captain of the guard in which Joseph was held. Both men held influential positions that demanded unwavering, unquestionable loyalty (see "Setting the Stage"). The cupbearer oversaw Pharaoh's drink, and the baker managed his food. These positions gave them immediate access to the king on a daily basis. These highly trusted servants may have even served as influential advisors.

Since Pharaoh was displeased with both at once, he may have gotten ill after a meal and suspected that one or both of them neglected their duties or purposely allowed him to be poisoned or eat spoiled food. Joseph's imprisonment in the "house of confinement" brought him in contact with these influential members of Pharaoh's court. Considering that the accusation by Potiphar's wife should have resulted in his execution—had Potiphar believed the charge—Joseph's interaction with Pharaoh's high-ranking servants while in prison shows that God was directing Joseph's path. God was paving the way for his rise to power.

Joseph was responsible for the well-being of the prisoners, including the cupbearer and baker (Gen 40:4), so when they reported their troubling dreams, he was ready to help. Both officials had been in custody for some time (the text literally says "days"), and both had ominous dreams on the same night (Gen 40:5). When Joseph "came to them in the morning" (Gen 40:6), they were anxious and confounded: They had no one to interpret their dreams. Confident that God would provide the interpretation, Joseph volunteered (Gen 40:8).

> **Quick Bit:** Almost all people in the ancient world attached some significance to dreams. The ancient Egyptians and Mesopotamians kept records of dreams and their interpretations for professional consultation. The biblical presentation of dreams and their interpretation aligns with this ancient Near Eastern context.

First, the cupbearer described his dream (Gen 40:9-11), in which he saw three branches, ripened grapes, and Pharaoh's cup. Joseph interpreted the dream to mean that the cupbearer would be freed and reinstated to his former position in three days.

After delivering good news to the cupbearer, Joseph saw an opportunity to encourage the cupbearer to use his restored influence with Pharaoh on Joseph's behalf. This scene contains the only dialogue in which Joseph reflects openly about his circumstances. In his brief remark, Joseph asked the cupbearer, "only remember me," emphasizing his status as a victim of injustice—both in terms of his brothers and Potiphar's wife (Gen 40:14-15). Having trusted God for the interpretation of the dream, Joseph does his best to take advantage of a God-given opportunity to plant a seed in the cupbearer's mind.

Joseph's positive message to the cupbearer inspired the baker to relate the details of his dream (Gen 40:16-17), in which he say three baskets of food on top of his head, with birds eating out of the top basket. Joseph explained that the baker's dream means bad news; he would be executed by Pharaoh in three days.

The Bible does not record either official's reaction, though we can imagine the cupbearer slept peacefully while the baker fretted for three days, hoping Joseph's interpretation would prove incorrect. The scene concludes with a matter-of-fact report of the events just as Joseph had predicted (Gen 40:21-22). The story of the servants and their enigmatic dreams served to showcase Joseph's God-given talent for interpreting dreams. That talent will prove essential to Joseph's eventual release and rise to power, but not before he spends two more years in custody: In the cupbearer's relief at surviving his ordeal, he forgets all about Joseph (Gen 40:23).

THROUGHOUT THE BIBLE

Joseph's life was marked by hostility, turmoil, and imprisonment—but his experience was not unique among the people of God. The Bible contains numerous examples of righteous people who suffered unjustly for their role of bringing about God's plan of redemption.

The story of the prophet Jeremiah relates closely to that of Joseph. Jeremiah 38 tells how Jeremiah, faithful to his office in King Zedekiah's court, prophesied about Israel's impending defeat at the hands of the Babylonians. If Israel would surrender and submit to the Babylonians, they would be spared:

> Thus says the LORD, Those who stay in this city shall die by the sword, by famine, and by pestilence; but those who go out to the Chaldeans shall live; they shall have their lives as a prize of war, and live. Thus says the LORD, This city shall surely be handed over to the army of the king of Babylon and be taken (Jer 38:2–3 NRSV).

But Jeremiah's message—God's message—enraged some of the officials in King Zedekiah's court. They reported that Jeremiah was discouraging the troops and persuaded the king to have Jeremiah cast into an empty cistern. The king, foreshadowing the actions of Pilate at the trial of Jesus (Matt 27:24), gave Jeremiah into their hands. Even though they were Judaean "brothers" of Jeremiah, the officials threw the prophet into a cistern, just like Joseph's brothers had done to him (Jer 38:6; Gen 37:24).

John the Baptist, the forerunner of Jesus, the Messiah (Matt 3), was also unjustly imprisoned because he spoke the unpopular words of God. John publicly opposed Herod's relationship with his brother's wife, Herodias: "For Herod, after arresting John, bound him and put him in prison on account of Herodias, the former wife of his brother Philip, because John had been saying to him, 'It is not permitted for you to have her' " (Matt 14:3–4). To spare himself the bad publicity of John's denouncement, Herod threw him in prison and eventually had him beheaded (Matt 14:10–11).

Joseph is the first in the long line of unjustly imprisoned servants of God. Although he was not a prophet, Joseph had the favor of God—especially when he was imprisoned. Genesis 39:2–5 tells us that "The LORD was with

Joseph" and caused him to prosper to such a degree that even Potiphar saw that Joseph's success was due to God's blessing. Again in Genesis 39:21–23 we see:

> The LORD was with Joseph and showed him steadfast love; he gave him favor in the sight of the chief jailer. The chief jailer committed to Joseph's care all the prisoners who were in the prison, and whatever was done there, he was the one who did it. The chief jailer paid no heed to anything that was in Joseph's care, because the LORD was with him; and whatever he did, the LORD made it prosper (NRSV).

Despite the suffering he endured, Joseph's fate differed from Jeremiah's and John's. As the story will show, following his imprisonment, Joseph was elevated to second in command of Pharaoh's kingdom. He lived out the remainder of his life in the splendor of the palace, providing generously for his family and preserving Egypt and the surrounding area during a terrible famine. But before he reached that height, Joseph endured years as a lowly servant and prisoner. Through it all, he resisted the temptation to become bitter or resentful toward God. He was able to persevere because he believed that God knew his circumstances and was directing his steps.

BEYOND THE BIBLE

Joseph's story shares many similarities and themes with Egyptian folklore. The tale of *Sinuhe* (pronounced sin-oo-he) tells the story of an Egyptian courtier who tended to the daily needs of the princess, the Pharaoh's daughter. When the Pharaoh died, the prince and the other royal sons who were away at war were summoned home. Before they arrived, Sinuhe overheard what he thought was a plot for a coup by one of the Pharaoh's other sons. Fearing he would be found out and killed by the plotter, Sinuhe fled Egypt and sought safety wherever he could find it.

Quick Bit: *Sinuhe* was composed during Egypt's Middle Kingdom or 11th Dynasty (ca. 2106–1963 BC), several centuries before the time of Joseph. The most accomplished work of prose literature of its time,[4] *Sinuhe* may have influenced how the biblical author organized Joseph's story.

Sinuhe settled in a foreign land. Other Egyptians in the area noticed of him and brought him to their king. After hearing him speak—and recognizing his intelligence and skill—the king gave him a position of prominence. Sinuhe tells the story:

> He set me at the head of his children. He married me to his eldest daughter. He let me choose for myself of his land, of the best that was his, on his border with another land.... Much also came to me because of the love of me; for he had made me chief of a tribe in the best part of his land.... I passed many years, my children becoming strong men, each a master of his tribe.... I gave water to the thirsty; I showed the way to him who had strayed; I rescued him who had been robbed.... I won [the king's] heart and he loved me, for he recognized my valor. He set me at the head of his children, for he saw the strength of my arms.[5]

Toward the end of his life, Sinuhe was welcomed home and reconciled with his former masters. His honor was restored, and he lived the remainder of his days in the palace.

Although the stories differ in the details, they reflect this same exile-restoration plot.[6] Against his will or desires, the main character travels to a foreign land and settles there. His god (or God) blesses him and grants him favor in the eyes of the foreign king. As a result of the hero's wisdom and skill—as well as divine blessing—he achieves a prominent place as a co-ruler of the foreign land. After some time, he is reconciled to his former life, and he lives the rest of his days in peace and prosperity—his reward for honorably persevering through the difficult circumstances he had to endure.

This exile-restoration plot is developed most poignantly in Joseph's story, and Genesis 40 marks the beginning of his reversal of fortune. Joseph's imprisonment gave way to the splendors of palace life. But unlike his counterparts in Egyptian lore, Joseph's newfound position of prominence was not merely a reward for his suffering and patient endurance; it was also the means by which God would bring about a great salvation.

APPLICATION

We all experience seasons of bitter disappointment or circumstances that seem to go from bad to worse. During these times we may struggle to detect God's work or presence in our lives. We may lose hope in God's plan or succumb to self-pity while we wait for God to rearrange the scenery. His call to us as believers, however, is to remain faithful even when his voice seems faint and his presence distant.

Joseph's response to suffering was to keep moving forward in the faith that God was going ahead of him. The Genesis narrative doesn't reveal all of Joseph's thoughts or actions during his imprisonment. It does focus on his continued reliance on God and God's gift of dream interpretation. It never leaves us in doubt about God's presence with Joseph, blessing him and his masters, providing true interpretations of the officials' dreams. As Joseph's story continues, we see how Joseph's imprisonment strengthened his character and increased his trust in God.

In Romans 5, Paul writes about how God uses suffering to create growth in our lives. According to Paul, we can rejoice in our sufferings because we know that "suffering produces endurance, and endurance produces character, and character produces hope" (Rom 5:4). This process helps us mature as Christians and gain wisdom from our past trials—but it does require our active participation.

Joseph knew all about trials. He suffered when his brothers sold him into slavery, but he endured to gain Potiphar's respect because of his godly character (Gen 39:2-4). Later, Joseph's commitment to God caused him not only to resist the advances of Potiphar's wife, but also to remain hopeful during a long and unjust imprisonment. In doing so, Joseph demonstrated the proper, though difficult, response to suffering: unwavering faith.

DISCUSSION

A Closer Look

1. The cupbearer and baker were imprisoned because Pharaoh believed they had violated his trust. Reflect on a time when your integrity or motivation was questioned due to circumstances beyond your control. How did you react?

_____

_____

_____

2. Joseph spends years in prison although he has done nothing wrong. Put yourself in his position. How would you feel after years of unjust imprisonment? What would your attitude toward God be like?

_____

_____

_____

Throughout the Bible

1. Can you think of other examples of God's people suffering unjustly? Were they ultimately vindicated? When?

_____

_____

_____

2. Why do you think God allows us to experience struggles and tests of character? What benefit do they serve in the lives of his followers?

_____

_____

_____

Beyond the Bible

1. What was God's ultimate purpose in bringing Joseph into Pharaoh's court? What does this communicate about the reason for Joseph's sufferings so far in the story?

_____

_____

_____

2. Why might the biblical authors have used the literature of the nations around them as a model for organizing their material? What does this communicate about their understanding of God's superiority over the gods of other nations?

_____

_____

_____

Application

1. What do you think Joseph did to maintain his hope during his time in prison? Which aspects of prison do you think were hardest for him?

_____

_____

_____

2. Recall a time of suffering in your life that produced character and hope. How can you use that experience to prepare for future trials?

_____

_____

_____

CHAPTER 4

POSITIONED WITH PURPOSE

Read Genesis 41:1–57.

SETTING THE STAGE

Theme. We cannot reach the end of a long journey in one great leap. We must take a step—and another step. Sometimes our path leads through rough terrain or takes frustrating detours. We may believe our ordeal will never end—and that we face it alone. But God never abandons his people. Although we can't see where he's leading, we can trust that he has a purpose for every steep climb and every valley. The times we find most difficult may be the very occasions God is positioning us where we need to be before he unfolds the next part of his plan.

Joseph endured an unjust imprisonment for more than two years. He must have wondered what God's purpose was during that time. In spite of his faithfulness to God, his troubles continued to drag on. Joseph could not see it what his life had in store, but God had a purpose. Every perceived setback actually brought Joseph one step closer to the fulfillment of God's purpose. In Genesis 41 we see how Joseph's perseverance finally paid off.

Literary Context. While in prison, Joseph interpreted a dream for Pharaoh's cupbearer, revealing that he would be restored to his position in Pharaoh's court just three days later (Gen 40:12-13). Joseph asked the cupbearer to tell Pharaoh about him and his unjust imprisonment, hoping Pharaoh would release him (Gen 40:14-15).

Three days later, true to Joseph's interpretation, Pharaoh restored the cupbearer to his former position (Gen 40:20-21). But relieved and busy with resuming his duties, the cupbearer forgot about Joseph (Gen 40:23). He languished in prison for two more years until Pharaoh himself needed an interpreter for his dreams. Genesis 41 traces Joseph's story, from Pharaoh's prisoner to his right-hand man, second in command over all of Egypt. The events in Genesis 41 also set the stage for the fulfillment of Joseph's dreams from Genesis 37—dreams in which his family would bow down to him as ruler over the land of Egypt (Gen 42:6). Dreams had sent Joseph into slavery; now dreams catapulted him into a position of great authority.

Historical & Cultural Background. Dreams and dream interpretation were very important in the ancient Near East—to the point that rules for understanding dreams were preserved in certain ancient Egyptian documents.[1] In certain cases, the interpreter was instructed to look for similarities between images in the dream and possible future scenarios. For example, looking into a deep well was thought to indicate that the dreamer would be imprisoned. In other cases, the interpreter was instructed to base the interpretation on a pun or wordplay. Along those lines, dreaming about a large cat (Egyptian *miu 'aa*) was believed to indicate a large harvest (Egyptian *shemu 'aa*).

The ancients believed a dream that occurred more than once was especially important. A Sumerian king who ruled around 2000 BC had two dreams instructing him to build a temple.[2] In the epic that bears his name, Gilgamesh had two dreams that foretold the coming of his companion and friend, Enkidu.[3] Another text from Mari indicates that having the same dream on consecutive nights made it even more significant.[4] So when Pharaoh had two dreams in the same night in Genesis 41:1-7, deciphering the meaning became especially urgent (Gen 41:32).

At that time dream interpreters usually took credit for the deciphering. But Joseph made it clear that his interpretations came from God (Gen 40:8; 41:16). When Pharaoh promoted Joseph, he also recognized that Joseph's insights originated with God (Gen 41:38-39).

With Pharaoh's promotion of Joseph, we begin to see God's purpose being accomplished. Joseph was 30 years old when Pharaoh released him from prison and appointed him over his house (Gen 41:46); thirteen years had passed since his brothers sold him as a slave (Gen 37:2). For almost half his life, Joseph had been a slave or a prisoner. But now his perseverance was about to pay off.

A CLOSER LOOK

Genesis 40 closes with the cupbearer being restored but neglecting to remember Joseph. Chapter 41 propels us two years ahead in Joseph's story. Although those two years were not recorded in Scripture, we can imagine how slowly that time passed for Joseph as he hoped for word from Pharaoh's court. We know he continued serving in the "house of confinement" and that he had as much freedom and responsibility as could be expected under the circumstances. After two years, however, Joseph likely gave up any hope that the cupbearer would remember him and petition Pharaoh on his behalf. Fortunately, something was about to jog the cupbearer's memory.

Like his servants two years prior, Pharaoh was beset by troubling dreams that he could not understand. The narrative opens by recounting these dreams (Gen 41:1–7). Pharaoh later repeats the details to Joseph (Gen 41:17–24). Such repetition seems to serve the literary purpose of ordering the story around pairs or doubles—two royal officials and their two dreams, the passage of two years, Pharaoh's two dreams each told twice, the repetition of the earlier dreams and their outcomes—all culminating in Genesis 41:32: "And the doubling of Pharaoh's dream [meant] that the thing [was] fixed by God, and God [would] shortly bring it about" (ESV). The repetition emphasizes the inevitability of what was about to happen; the matter was established, God had already decided. In other words, Joseph's interpretation will surely come to pass.

Quick Bit: Who is Pharaoh in this story? The books of Genesis and Exodus never mention the name of any Egyptian king. In fact, the Bible doesn't mention the names of any Egyptian king until the time of Solomon (see 1 Kgs 11:40. There are three possible historical settings for the Joseph story: The Hysksos period (1750–1550 BC), the Amarna period (ca. 1375–1350 BC), or the Middle Kingdom (ca. 2000–1750 BC). The first two periods saw an increase in the Semitic population in Egypt, and records confirm that Semitic people were appointed to Egyptian offices.[5] The Bible's chronology, however, suggests Joseph's story occurred during the Middle Kingdom, when Semitic people traded with Egypt and settled in the area. But the available evidence is not enough to specifically identify the era or the pharaoh in this story.

Pharaoh may have had other dreams during the two years since the cupbearer's return to court, but they must not have troubled him or defied explanation like those of Genesis 41. In his first dream, Pharaoh saw seven fat cows and seven gaunt cows emerging from the Nile River (Gen 41:1-2). The thin cows swallowed the fat cows—an image disturbing enough to rouse him from sleep (Gen 41:3). In the second, he dreamt of seven plump ears of grain being devoured by seven withered ears of grain (Gen 41:5-7). The sense of foreboding and imminent disaster, punctuated by the grotesque and unnatural imagery, deeply unsettled Pharaoh. Fraught with anxiety, he immediately sought an explanation.

Pharaoh's wise men and magicians were at a loss to explain the dreams (Gen 41:8). Since dream interpretation was part of their professional repertoire, Pharaoh likely became angry at their failure. He still lacked an interpretation for his troublesome dreams. At that moment, when the cupbearer overheard the exchange, he recalled his own experience with Joseph. He quickly explained to Pharaoh how he came to know a Hebrew slave with an uncanny ability to interpret dreams (Gen 41:9-13). The cupbearer's clipped account—we dreamed, he interpreted, it happened—prompted Pharaoh to action. He immediately brought Joseph out of prison (Gen 41:12-14).

In Genesis 41:14, the narrative uses the Hebrew word *bor*, meaning "pit," likely an intentional link to Genesis 37:24—the beginning of Joseph's ordeal. The word also echoes Joseph's own words in Genesis 40:15 where he alludes to his past troubles of being kidnapped and unjustly confined in a "pit." Joseph's story pivots on this reversal of fortune. His early dreams of authority over his family tumbled him into the pit—his long ordeal of slavery and imprisonment. Now, Pharaoh's dreams pull him out of the pit and it initiates the fulfillment of his dreams.

Following Egyptian custom, Joseph was shaved and dressed in clothes appropriate for an audience with the Pharaoh (Gen 41:14). Egyptians typically shaved their heads and beards, whereas Semitic peoples were generally bearded and associated baldness and shaving with shame and grief (Amos 8:10; Job 1:20). The physical transformation turned Joseph into an Egyptian, making him unrecognizable as a Hebrew foreigner and son of Jacob (Gen 42:8).

With Joseph's arrival, Pharaoh wasted no words: He explained that Joseph's ability to interpret dreams had come to his attention and that he was in need of those services (Gen 41:15). Joseph refused to take any credit for his interpretations—a response that likely surprised Pharaoh (Gen 41:16). Joseph faithfully proclaimed that God alone was responsible for the interpretations, just as he did earlier with the cupbearer and baker (Gen 40:8). Pharaoh then recounted his dreams (Gen 41:17-24), yet he added a new detail: the consumption of the fat cows by the gaunt cows did not change the appearance of the bony, underfed cows (Gen 41:21).

Joseph then revealed their meaning, indicating that both dreams pointed to the same future: seven years of plenty would be followed by seven years of famine (Gen 41:25-32). As Joseph's words indicated, God chose to reveal the future to Pharaoh—not because he could prevent it, but so he could prepare for it. Joseph then went beyond Pharaoh's request for an interpretation of the dreams. Without hesitating or giving Pharaoh a chance to respond, Joseph advised him on what he must do to deal with the impending crisis (Gen 41:33-36). Joseph treated the interpretation as an absolute certainty demanding immediate action.

Joseph recommended that Egypt's agricultural affairs be placed under the oversight of a "discerning and wise" man who would manage the surplus from the good years to create a reserve food supply for the bad years. Joseph's advice was neutral, based only on the needs of the situation; his words contained no hint of self-recommendation for the job. The careful reader, however, may notice the subtle implication that Pharaoh's "wise" men—who failed to interpret the dreams—were not wise enough for this role (Gen 41:33). Indeed, Pharaoh recognized this and declared that they would find no one more "discerning and wise" than Joseph himself (Gen 41:39).

Pharaoh promoted Joseph on the spot—apparently making him second-in-command over all the land of Egypt (Gen 41:40). Pharaoh also invested Joseph with the symbols of his high office: the royal signet ring, a gold chain, and public acclamation of his authority in Pharaoh's second chariot (Gen 41:42–43). Joseph's acceptance of the office and Pharaoh's agreement to Joseph's plan are quietly and quickly assumed in the narrative.

> **Quick Bit:** Joseph's promotion contains several details that can be checked against Egyptian historical and cultural sources. The signet ring or royal seal, the linen garments, and the gold chains are well documented symbols of formal investiture.[6] Joseph's possession of Pharaoh's seal reflects the Egyptian office of "Royal Seal Bearer"—a title often held by the vizier or prime minister. Joseph's prominent position as second only to Pharaoh in authority (Gen 41:40) indicates that he may have been the prime minister—in charge of all administrative matters in the kingdom after Pharaoh. Or Joseph could have been second to Pharaoh in a particular sphere of influence, such as minister over agricultural affairs.

Joseph's assimilation into Egyptian society became complete when he received an Egyptian name and married into a prominent Egyptian family (Gen 41:45). Joseph was given the name "Zaphenath-paneah," which probably means "God speaks and he lives."[7] Joseph married Asenath, the daughter of an Egyptian priest from the religious center of On (or Heliopolis) where the Egyptian sun gods were worshiped. While the narrative refrains from passing judgment on Joseph's acceptance of an Egyptian bride, it never mentions her again except as the mother of Joseph's two sons (Gen 41:50–52). It also never refers to Joseph by his Egyptian name. While Joseph's prominent position in Egyptian society was important for God's ultimate purpose for Israel, the focus remains on his connection with Israel, not on his new life in Egypt.

Joseph began work immediately. The seven years of plenty came just as he said they would, and Joseph organized the effort to gather the surplus grain (Gen 41:47–49). At the end of seven years, the storehouses overflowed with the excess, and Joseph's reputation for administrative leadership was firmly established.

> **Quick Bit:** The names Joseph chooses for his two sons reflect his attitude about his new life in Egypt. He calls his first son Manasseh—a pun on the Hebrew word meaning "cause to forget"—explaining

that God has helped him to forget his separation from his family (Gen 41:51). He names his second son Ephraim, which relates to the Hebrew verb meaning "be fruitful," explaining that "God has made me fruitful in the land of my misfortune" (Gen 41:52). These names emphasize his acceptance of God's blessing even in the midst of his personal struggles.

When the famine came, Egypt found itself well prepared, thanks to Joseph's planning. The famine affected Egypt and all the surrounding countries, so Joseph's abundant store of food came into high demand throughout the region. Everyone had to go through Joseph to purchase grain from Egypt—even nomadic shepherds from Canaan, who were also hit hard by the famine.

THROUGHOUT THE BIBLE

After enduring years of undeserved imprisonment, Joseph found himself at the pinnacle of power in Egypt. The narrative of Joseph's experience in Egypt eventually developed into a motif in Jewish history. His story not only became an example for later Jews; it served as a narrative form for telling similar stories of God's providence and faithfulness for Jews in foreign contexts.

These stories begin with a non-Jewish king having a dream. After much confusion and mental anguish, the king calls his wise men to interpret the dream for him, but none are able. After exhausting all available resources, a member of the king's court recommends the services of a foreigner. This foreigner is a Jew and is typically a prisoner or exile. The Jewish hero gives God the credit for his skill and interprets the troubled king's dream. As a reward, the king elevates the Jewish hero to a position of prominence and authority in his court, often making him a co-ruler. The hero lives out the remainder of his days in the foreign palace without compromising the distinctiveness of his Jewish faith. He is viewed by all as a model of fidelity, virtue, and wisdom.

This narrative form most clearly plays out in the account of Daniel. The story begins with Nebuchadnezzar's destruction of Jerusalem and captivity of the Jews. Among those taken into exile were Daniel and his three friends, who were quickly set apart for their superior skill and wisdom (Dan 1:20). As the story progresses, King Nebuchadnezzar has a dream that troubles him deeply (Dan 2:1). He summons the wise men, but no one can tell him the meaning of his dream (Dan 2:2–11). In anger and frustration, Nebuchadnezzar commands that all the wise men be killed (Dan 2:12).

Because Daniel and his three friends are among the wise men, they, too, find themselves facing death. But Daniel tells Arioch, the servant in charge of carrying out Nebuchadnezzar's commands, that he can interpret Nebuchadnezzar's dream (Dan 2:24). Arioch reports to Nebuchadnezzar, "I have found a man among the exiles of Judah who can relate the explanation to the king" (Dan 2:25). Brought before the king, Daniel immediately gives God the credit for his ability:

> The mystery that the king asks, no wise men, conjurers, magicians, or diviners are able to make known to the king. But there is a God in heaven who reveals mysteries, and he has made known to King Nebuchadnezzar what it is that will be at the end of days (Dan 2:27–28).

After telling the king both his dream and its interpretation, Daniel is elevated to a position of high honor in the court (Dan 2:48). The king recognizes God's providential action in Daniel's life and credits God with the honor he deserves: "Truly your God is the God of gods and the Lord of kings, and he reveals mysteries, for you are able to reveal this mystery" (Dan 2:47).

True to form, Daniel's career in the court of a foreign king follows the same pattern as Joseph's. God's sovereignty propels the dramatic development and resolution in both stories. Both Daniel and Joseph stand in awe of God's character—as do the foreigners in whose courts they serve. Nebuchadnezzar tells Daniel, "Truly your God is the God of gods and the Lord of kings" (Dan 2:47). Pharaoh likewise recognized that Joseph was a man "in whom is the spirit of God" (Gen 41:38).

BEYOND THE BIBLE

To help establish Joseph in Egyptian society, he was given an Egyptian wife named Asenath (Gen 41:45). She was the daughter of Potiphera, priest of On (or Heliopolis)—an important cultic city. Although this advantageous marriage elevated Joseph's status among the Egyptian elite, it has long troubled readers that Joseph, a model of virtue, would marry the daughter of a pagan priest.

A legend called *Joseph and Asenath* attempts to deal with this discrepancy. Composed sometime between the first century BC and second century AD, *Joseph and Asenath* presents the marriage in a way that upholds Joseph's piety and overcomes the difficulty of Asenath's pagan heritage. The story describes Asenath as an exceedingly beautiful and arrogant woman: "[S]he was tall as Sarah and handsome as Rebecca and beautiful as Rachel."[8] The text goes on: "And Asenath was despising and scorning every man, and she was boastful and arrogant with everyone."[9] It also describes her as an idolater, a reasonable conclusion given her father's priestly office in the Egyptian court: "And within [her] chamber gods of the Egyptians who were without number were fixed to the walls, even gods of gold and silver. And Asenath worshiped them all and feared them and performed sacrifices to them every day."[10]

> **Quick Bit:** *Joseph and Asenath* also creatively tells a story of rebellion instigated by Pharaoh's son. Following Joseph and Asenath's marriage, Pharaoh's son saw Asenath and desired to marry her. He plotted with some of Joseph's brothers to kill Pharaoh and Joseph, take Asenath as his queen, and assume Egypt's throne. When the coup failed, Asenath forgave Joseph's brothers. Pharaoh's son died, followed by his grieving father, who left his throne to Joseph. Joseph then ruled Egypt for 48 years before his death.

During the first year of plenty (Gen 41:47–49), as Joseph traveled throughout Egypt gathering grain, he told Potiphera that he would visit his house and requested to dine there. Knowing of Joseph's great fame and reputation, Potiphera told Asenath—who had refused all other suitors—that Pharaoh would give her to Joseph as a wife. Incensed, she refused her father's wishes and scorned Joseph. She left when she heard that Joseph was approaching the dining hall. But when she saw Joseph through a window, she fell madly in love with him. She returned to the dining hall and greeted Joseph with a kiss. But Joseph refused her and said:

It is not fitting for a man who worships God, who will bless with his mouth the living God and eat blessed bread of life and drink a blessed cup of immortality, and anoint himself with blessed oint-ment of incorruptibility, to kiss a strange woman who will bless with her mouth dead and dumb idols and eat from their table bread of strangulation, and drink from their libation a cup of insidious-ness, and anoint herself with ointment of destruction.[11]

Joseph then prayed for Asenath, telling Potiphera that he would return in eight days. Asenath was deeply convicted and spent the week mourning and fasting, repenting of her arrogance and idolatry. "And she wept with great and bitter weeping and repented of her infatuation with the gods whom she used to worship, and spurned all the idols...."[12] She smashed her idols and threw them out of her window. In sackcloth and ashes, she sat by herself, locked in her chamber, and prayed to God:

> With you I take refuge, Lord,
> and to you I will shout, Lord,
> to you I will pour out my supplication,
> to you I will confess my sins,
> and to you I will reveal my lawless deeds.
> Spare me, Lord,
> because I have sinned much before you,
> I have committed lawlessness and irreverence,
> and have said wicked and unspeakable things before you.[13]

In response to her repentance, an angel came and assured her of God's ac-ceptance and her forthcoming marriage to Joseph. She adorned herself as a bride and, when Joseph returned, the two were wed by Pharaoh in the royal palace. They lived out their lives as advocates of the one true God in the midst of pagan idolaters.

This ancient story teaches us something we already know from the biblical text: Joseph refused to compromise his trust and faith in God. We shouldn't be bothered that he was rewarded with Asenath as a wife; throughout his story—and at its conclusion—Joseph recognized that God was orchestrat-ing the events of his life to save many people (Gen 50:20). Potiphera and Egypt's gods had nothing to do with it, nor did they influence what was to come as the details of God's plan became clearer in Genesis 41.

APPLICATION

When we need encouragement to endure difficult times while trusting in God's plan, we can find inspiration in Genesis 40–41 and the story of Joseph. These two chapters illustrate how to endure hardship while maintaining trust, and they demonstrate how faithful perseverance paves the way for God to work his divine plan through our lives. Joseph's patient endurance leads to blessing—for himself, his family, Egypt, all those caught by famine, and the future nation of Israel. Had he not been imprisoned—wrongly, for standing true to his faith—Joseph may never have risen to prominence in Pharaoh's court. God orchestrates our circumstances for his glory and his purpose. But we must be faithful and obedient to see those plans come to fruition.

It can be an immense struggle to maintain our patience and continue to walk in faith before others—especially when our hardship stems from others treating us unfairly because of our faith. Joseph must have wondered whether God would ever deliver him from prison. Although he could interpret dreams, he couldn't possibly anticipate how God's plan would unfold. But God often gives us a glimpse of his hand in our lives. Joseph earned favor, both in Potiphar's house and in prison, due to his loyal service and God's provision. He was able to interpret the dreams of Pharaoh's officials because God gave him the interpretations. No matter his circumstances—and no matter our own—we can see God working in our lives if we have the faith to look. Those glimpses of God's hand help us remain confident in his goodness and mercy.

The psalmists clearly grasped this concept. Psalm 37 urges "commit your way to the LORD; trust in him, and he will act. He will bring forth your righteousness as the light, and your justice as the noonday" (Psa 37:5–6, ESV). As we learn in Joseph's story, part of waiting on God involves waiting on *his* timing. While we long for immediate deliverance, James tells us "blessed is the man who remains steadfast under trial, for when he has stood the test he will receive the crown of life, which God has promised to those who love him" (Jas 1:12). Joseph reminds us that even when it's difficult to discern God's hand in our lives, he continues to work out his plan in his time.

DISCUSSION

A Closer Look

1. God's blessing and Joseph's initiative are both instrumental in God's plan. How can we use our gifts to be the means for God's working in the world?

_____

_____

_____

2. Joseph was thankful and faithful in the midst of discouraging circumstances. How does discouragement present a challenge for our faith to overcome?

_____

_____

_____

Throughout the Bible

1. What other examples of Jews succeeding in a foreign court can you think of?

_____

_____

_____

2. What further lessons could Jews in exile learn from Joseph's example?

_____

_____

_____

Beyond the Bible

1. What platform has God given you to make his message known? How are you accomplishing this?

_____

_____

_____

2. Why do you think Pharaoh changed Joseph's name and gave him an Egyptian wife? What was he trying to accomplish? Did it work?

_____

_____

_____

Application

1. Imagine yourself in Joseph's circumstances. Do you think you could have endured as he did?

_____

_____

_____

2. When challenged by hardship and trial, what verses remind you of God's providence and sovereign care? Why?

_____

_____

_____

CHAPTER 5

GRAPPLING WITH GUILT

Read Genesis 42:1–38.

SETTING THE STAGE

Theme. Guilt is such a powerful emotion that many of us struggle to overcome it. Even though God has granted us his forgiveness, the weight of past sins can hinder us from living in the freedom that comes with full recognition of God's grace. And not just past struggles—ongoing ones can bind us as well. It's difficult to silence our mind's whisper that our failures and struggles make us unable or unworthy to serve God.

When we encounter Joseph's brothers again, we find them prisoners of guilt due to their crime against him. Twenty years have passed since they dropped their brother in a pit and condemned him to a life of slavery. But when they travel to Egypt to find relief from the famine, the brothers encounter a brash Egyptian official. Although they fail to recognize him as Joseph, the way he treats them immediately compels them to wonder if God is punishing them for their sin against their brother (see Gen 42:21, 22, 28). They could not yet see that God was using their treacherous act for his greater purpose—a divine work they will only later recognize and understand.

Literary Context. Genesis 42 recalls many of the details from the beginning of Joseph's story. As Joseph's brothers prostrate themselves to him in Egypt (Gen 42:6), we recall the stalks of wheat that bowed to Joseph in his youthful dream (Gen 37:5–8). Standing before his humbled brothers,

Joseph "remember[s] the dreams he had dreamed of them," and his life comes full circle—past and present connecting (Gen 42:9). Although he has been absent from his brothers' lives for two decades, they have not forgotten him. Caught off guard by the resistance of this Egyptian official, the brothers repeatedly refer to their sin of selling Joseph into slavery (Gen 42:21–22, 28, 32). The story set in motion in Genesis 37 now begins to play out for Joseph's brothers.

Throughout the progressions in Joseph's story, we continue to witness God's providential unfolding of his purpose. As Joseph had interpreted earlier, Pharaoh's dream was fulfilled, and Egypt experienced seven years of plentiful harvests followed by seven years of drought (Gen 41:47–49). Thanks to Joseph's amassing of a surplus of grain during the seven years of plenty, Egypt's stockpiles could provide not only for its population, but also for the peoples from surrounding regions. The famine leaves Joseph's humbled, downtrodden brothers no option but to travel to Egypt in search of grain.

Historical & Cultural Background. Joseph's face-to-face encounter with his brothers does not present us with the reunion we might expect. Instead of welcoming them with tearful embraces—or a rage-filled threat—Joseph accuses his brothers of being spies. Such an accusation against a group of Canaanites would not have been unusual. In the ancient world, it was a fairly common military practice to send in a few men as spies to gauge the strengths and weaknesses of the enemy (see Num 13:1–24). As a result, ancient Egyptians stationed guards at their northeastern border to watch for signs of espionage. Egypt's surplus of grain in Joseph's day probably made them a target for the region's impoverished nations.

The ancient Egyptians also had a fairly low opinion of Canaanites in general. They considered them to be uncivilized and untrustworthy.[1] Several ancient Egyptian texts also record complaints about the tendency of Canaanites to seek solace in Egypt during times of hardship. "The Prophecies of Neferti"—composed in the 20th century BC—describes Canaanite refugees, or "Asiatics," in particularly negative terms:

> The land is burdened with misfortune
> Because of those looking for food,
> Asiatics[2] roaming the land.

Foes have arisen in the east,
Asiatics have descended into Egypt.[3]

Another 20th century BC document, "The Instructions of Merikare," describes Canaanite travelers as untrustworthy:

Lo, the miserable Asiatic,
He is wretched because of the place he's in:
Short of water, bare of wood,
Its paths are many and painful because of mountains.
He does not dwell in one place,
Food propels his legs,
He fights since the time of Horus,
Not conquering nor being conquered,
He does not announce the day of combat,
Like a thief who darts about a group.[4]

Now a respected Egyptian official, Joseph had to decide the most appropriate way to behave toward these "detestable" Canaanite travelers—as a suspicious official or as a wronged brother. Yet, rather than encountering the jealous, spiteful men who sold him into slavery, Joseph met men paralyzed by decades of guilt (Gen 42:21). Observing his brothers in distress over the past, Joseph recognized that he was not the only one who had suffered.

A CLOSER LOOK

As famine consumed the land, Joseph's father, Jacob, encountered the same decision his grandfather, Abraham, faced so many years before: either purchase food in Egypt or starve in the land of promise (see Gen 12:10). But unlike Abraham, Jacob did not solve the dilemma by moving his entire household to Egypt. Perhaps remembering God's warning to Isaac against traveling to Egypt during a time of famine (Gen 26:1–2), Jacob sent 10 of his 11 sons to buy grain in Egypt and bring it back to Canaan (Gen 42:2).

Quick Bit: In Genesis, Egypt often symbolizes separation from God—a land outside of God's plan for his chosen people. In Genesis 12, Abraham's journey to Egypt seems to involve his turning from the promised land just after having arrived there. God intervenes to thwart Isaac's plan to leave Canaan for Egypt because of famine (Gen 26:1–2). These stories anticipate the bondage Israel will endure at Egyptian hands. After the Israelites endure the exodus, it becomes imperative to God's people to avoid Egypt at all costs (Deut 17:16; 28:68; Exod 14:13; Jer 42:15–19). Yet, in Joseph's story, God uses Egypt as the means to sustain his people through famine.

Still haunted by the loss of Joseph, Jacob kept Benjamin, his youngest son (and Joseph's full brother), home with him because he "feared harm would come to him" (Gen 42:4). As Rachel's second son, Benjamin ascended to the position of favorite after Jacob's loss of Joseph. Yet, Jacob's concern for Benjamin's safety was excessive. Benjamin was likely in his twenties at this point—older than Joseph was when Jacob sent him unaccompanied to find his brothers (Gen 37:2, 13) tending flocks in Dothan. Nonetheless Jacob responded to the loss of Joseph by restricting Benjamin's freedom. Afraid of losing his last connection to Rachel, he would not allow his youngest son out of his immediate care.

In Genesis 37, Jacob sent Joseph to find his brothers, which eventually resulted in Joseph's enslavement (Gen 37:12–14). Now, in sending his sons to Egypt, Jacob unknowingly sends them to Joseph. Undoubtedly the 10 brothers were among a much larger group making the journey to Egypt in search of relief from the famine. Joseph's brothers were 10 anonymous faces in a ceaseless stream of foreigners seeking food. When they stood before the official responsible for the food supplies in Egypt, they unwittingly stood before Joseph. They bowed to the ground out of desperation and respect for the official and power over their lives (Gen 42:6). But even after 20 years, Joseph recognized them immediately. Understanding their actions as a sign of total submission and deference, he undoubtedly knew that his first dream was being fulfilled in that moment (Gen 37:5–8; 42:9).

In that dream, Joseph and his brothers were harvesting grain when their sheaves bowed down to his (Gen 37:7). Now it was grain that brought his brothers to Egypt to bow before him, grain that he possessed and they so desperately needed. They bowed in recognition of his office, but they failed to recognize him, and he "pretended to be a stranger to them" (Gen 42:7). After 20 years, the same men who engineered his descent into slavery and isolation stood before him, vulnerable and dependent on him for survival.

Joseph initially responded by speaking roughly to them, interrogating them about their origins and accusing them of being spies (Gen 42:7, 9). The narrative does not disclose his motives for this behavior—whether he acts befitting his office so as not to lose face in front of his Egyptian subjects, whether he intends to take revenge against his brothers, or whether he is preparing for the moment in which he will revel in his dream coming true.

The scene is heavy with irony due to the reversal of fortune: The men bowing before him sold him into slavery, but their evil intentions led him to this position of great power—a position that can save them or destroy them. As a young man, Joseph was subject to his brothers' power and harsh treatment; now they are subject to his. Most of the trials Joseph inflicts on his brothers in Genesis 42-44 parallel their treatment of him in Genesis 37. Joseph fell victim to his brothers' revenge in Genesis 37:13 after previously giving a "bad report" to Jacob about them (Gen 37:2). Now Joseph turns the tables, accusing them of being spies.

The irony grows as the brothers protest that they are "honest men" and Joseph's "servants" (Gen 42:11). The last time we saw the brothers, they were deceiving their father about Joseph's fate—convincing him that Joseph had been killed by a wild animal (Gen 37:31-33). Now they appeal to their honest character in a desperate effort to exonerate themselves. Joseph ignores their pleas and repeats the accusation (Gen 42:14). To the other Egyptians present, Joseph's suspicion would not have appeared unusual, as Egyptians distrusted Canaanites and considered them to be uncivilized and untrustworthy (see "Setting the Stage"). They would have considered it completely reasonable to suspect that the brothers were scouting the storehouse for a raid. Joseph played on this distrust to put his brothers on edge.

In an attempt to prove their honesty, the brothers recount their family history—only this time they tell the truth. In fact, they offer Joseph more details than necessary to explain why only 10 of Jacob's 12 sons are present: The youngest remains at home, and the 12th is gone (Gen 42:13). Later, their father will scold them for this, asking, "Why did you bring trouble to me by telling the man you still had a brother?" (Gen 43:6). Once more we see the irony of the scene, as these "honest men" are again dishonest: They volunteer this information to Joseph, but upon recounting the events to their father, they claim that the Egyptian official forced them to divulge the detail by asking specifically about their father and whether they had any other brothers (Gen 43:7).

The extra detail provides Joseph with the basis for his test: He demands that the youngest brother appear before him to verify their account (Gen 42:15). Since Joseph knows they are telling the truth about their father having 12 sons, this ruse seems designed both to verify Benjamin's well-being and to test the brothers' concern for one of their own. Knowing how brutally they had treated him when *he* was Jacob's favorite, Joseph may have doubted their explanation of Benjamin's absence. Ultimately, he wanted to see Benjamin with his own eyes.

Joseph initially demanded that one brother fetch the youngest while the others remained in Egyptian custody (Gen 42:15-16). After holding the brothers for three days, he changed the plan: He required that only one brother remain in custody while the other nine returned with grain for their families. They were then to return with Benjamin to prove their honesty or else suffer death (Gen 42:19-20).

Hearing this, the brothers began to talk among themselves, assuming that Joseph could not understand them. Even though 20 years had passed since they sold Joseph into slavery, the brothers immediately connected their present plight with their past behavior, agonizing over how they ignored Joseph's pleas for mercy when they sold him (Gen 42:21). Reuben reminded them that he warned them against harming Joseph, and that they had failed to listen (Gen 42:22). Throughout their exchange, Joseph watched and listened until, overwhelmed by their admission of guilt, he turned to weep (Gen 42:23-24). After composing himself, he returned and chose Simeon to be imprisoned. He would only release Simeon after they returned with Benjamin to prove their story was true.

Here again we see a reversal between Joseph's treatment of his brothers and their earlier treatment of him. Decades before, the brothers could have killed Joseph—and initially they intended to do so. Now, with all but Simeon released, Joseph would expose their true character through this test. Would they abandon Simeon to slavery and imprisonment as they had abandoned him?[5]

Although Joseph claimed to be testing his brothers' honesty (Gen 42:15), his actions here can be interpreted two ways since the narrative does not provide a clear motive. Was Joseph simply testing his brothers' character to see if they had changed? Or was he taking revenge on his brothers by causing them distress? When he slips his money into his brother's bags before they leave for Canaan, did he act out of generosity or a sadistic desire to terrify them further (Gen 42:25)? The brothers failed to notice this unexpected refund until they were at least a day into their journey home. They panicked at the discovery, interpreting their misfortune as further retribution for their sins against Joseph (Gen 42:27–28). They react with a trembling cry: "What is this that God has done to us?" Surely they had committed other sins, but their treatment of Joseph loomed large in their collective conscience beyond forgiveness.

Joseph's brothers trudged home, laden with the knowledge that they must report to their father what had happened. Their tale parallels Genesis 37, which also ends with the brothers telling Jacob of the tragic fate of his son (Gen 37:32). This time, however, the fate of two sons—not just one–hangs in the balance. As they concluded their report, it seemed that Simeon was as good as lost (Gen 42:29–34). Despite the request of the Egyptian official, Jacob flatly refused to part with Benjamin (Gen 42:36). Now he had lost two sons—Joseph and Simeon. He would not give up another, regardless of the circumstances. Even after Reuben attempted to offer a guarantee—the lives of his own two sons if he failed to return with Benjamin alive—Jacob still refused to allow his youngest son to travel to Egypt (Gen 42:37–38). Jacob understood that his decision condemned Simeon to imprisonment and slavery, but the alternative—losing Benjamin forever—was unthinkable.

THROUGHOUT THE BIBLE

We usually know when our behavior is sin. Most of the sins we commit start with willful decisions to violate God's truth. But rarely do we stop and think about God's wrath and judgment before we confess and trust in God's forgiveness. The ancients had a much different idea of how their actions affected their standing before God.

As Joseph's brothers' encountered resistance from him in Egypt, they believed God was finally punishing them for the sins of their youth. They believed in a causal relationship between their past action and the difficulties they now encountered as they bowed at the feet of the Egyptian official. When Joseph said he would hold Simeon until they returned with Benjamin, they spoke among themselves:

> "Alas, we are paying the penalty for what we did to our brother; we saw his anguish when he pleaded with us, but we would not listen. That is why this anguish has come upon us" (Gen 42:21 NRSV).

Their perspective reflected an ancient Near Eastern concept of divine retribution. Reuben's response to their outburst brings this into even greater focus.

> "Did I not tell you not to wrong the boy? But you would not listen. So now there comes a reckoning for his blood" ... At this they lost heart and turned trembling to one another, saying, "What is this that God has done to us?" (Gen 42:22, 28 NRSV).

The notion that people get what they deserve—that there is a cause-and-effect relationship to every action—was common in Joseph's day. It is also reflected throughout the Bible. For example, in the book of Job, Job's three friends claimed that he experienced great calamity because of his sin:

> Is not your fear of God your confidence,
> and the integrity of your ways your hope?
> Think now, who that was innocent ever perished?
> Or where were the upright cut off?
> As I have seen, those who plow iniquity
> and sow trouble reap the same.
> By the breath of God they perish,
> and by the blast of his anger they are consumed (Job 4:6–9 NRSV).

According to their understanding of God's justice, those who do evil suffer, while those who act righteously find reward. Job's friends believed his suffering to be the result of personal failing—an argument they rehearse throughout the book (see Job 8:3–6).[6] The book of Proverbs also contains this concept of divine retribution (Prov 11:31; 13:21).

Yet this understanding fails to acknowledge God's freedom to exercise his grace and mercy. Pointing to a cause-and-effect relationship between good behavior and blessing is valuable when encouraging right behavior. But this perspective fails to recognize God's supremacy over all principles, and his freedom to act in the way he chooses—a fact Job's story powerfully illustrates.

Jesus' disciples raised this issue in John 9:2 concerning a man blind from birth: "Rabbi, who sinned, this man or his parents, that he should be born blind?" They believed the man's suffering had to be the result of someone's sin. Jesus' response aimed to break their assumption that suffering is always caused by sinful action. He told them, "It was not that this man sinned, or his parents, but that the works of God might be displayed in him" (John 9:3 ESV). The purpose of the man's affliction was to glorify God, which Jesus promptly brought about by restoring his sight (John 9:6–7).

When Joseph was a young man, his brothers committed a great evil against him. Now they believed their misfortune to be divine retribution (Gen 41:21–22, 28). Their guilt over selling the brother into slavery had eaten away at them for years, and they saw their present circumstances as payback. As for Joseph, he finally had the chance to get even. But as we will see, God's sovereign purpose will prompt Joseph to act as an agent of grace.

BEYOND THE BIBLE

When famine hit the region, God provided Joseph with the necessary wisdom and administrative skills to navigate an overwhelming natural disaster. But the task wasn't easy. Even with God's blessing, Joseph had the colossal responsibility of satisfying the hungry cries of the people (Gen 41:55). In traveling to Egypt, his brothers were simply doing what the rest of the world was doing: seeking relief from the famine (Gen 41:57).

Ancient texts can help us understand the oppressive conditions of famines in the ancient Near East. One in particular, *The Famine Stela*, tells the story of a pharaoh, King Djoser, who ruled through a seven-year famine. The disaster caused many of his people to suffer and die, and it devastated his kingdom.

> Grain was scant,
> Kernels were dried up,
> Scarce was every kind of food.
> Every man robbed his twin,
> Those who entered did not go.
> Children cried,
> Youngsters fell,
> The hearts of the old were grieving;
> Legs drawn up, they hugged the ground,
> Their arms clasped about them.
> Courtiers were needy,
> Temples were shut,
> Shrines covered with dust,
> Everyone was in distress.[7]

King Djoser sought the advice of a priest, who told him about the god Khnum who controlled the flow of the Nile River. Later, Khnum appeared to King Djoser in a dream and promised relief from the famine. The king responded gratefully and issued a decree granting Khnum's temple a share of the royal revenue. He entrusted a governor—like Joseph—with carrying out his edict.[8]

Quick Bit: *The Famine Stela* is an example of pseudepigrapha—an anonymous work claiming to be written by a famous figure from the past for the sake of gaining authority. It was originally thought to date to the time of King Djoser of Egypt (ca. 2650 BC), but its contents reflect the situation of the priesthood at the Khnum temple in the second-century BC. The authors of the document claimed it had been written by an ancient pharaoh to lend authority to its content.

The Famine Stela has many remarkable parallels to the Joseph story. As one scholar notes, "The similarity of the tale to the famine story of Genesis is quite striking, not only because of its Egyptian setting and seven-year famine but also because of the motifs of taxation (Gen 41:33–49; 47:13–26), dream omens (Gen 41:1–32), and preservation of priestly land

(Gen 47:22)."[9] These similarities have inspired discussion among scholars about whether the Joseph story influenced the writing of the stela.

Ultimately, both the biblical text and the stela communicate the devastating effects of famine and drought on the ancient populations of the Middle and Near East. But in Joseph's story, God used this natural disaster to bring deliverance and salvation. The famine not only generated the context for the reunion and preservation of Joseph's family, it also set the stage for the greatest example of God's deliverance in the OT—the exodus from Egypt.

APPLICATION

We often struggle under the weight of guilt and shame, which isn't entirely surprising since we have all sinned against others and God. Yet when we ignore or suppress our sins, we complicate matters by failing to resolve them, which can cause even greater damage.

By the time Joseph's brothers traveled to Egypt, they could have forgotten him altogether, choosing to suppress the memories of their treachery against their father's favorite. Yet when Joseph asked to see their youngest brother, they were overwhelmed with guilt. All this time, they had been concealing past sin. Consumed by subconscious guilt, they lived in fear of repercussions, holding to a distorted image of a vengeful God (Gen 42:28; see also 44:16).

As believers, we can take comfort in knowing that the grace God extends to us through Christ frees us from the burden of sin (Rom 8:1). But unlike Joseph's brothers, we should respond to sin not based on our feelings of shame, but based on a desire for communion with God.

God *already* knows the depths of our hearts—what we have done, thought, and said. As the author of Hebrews writes, "no creature is hidden in the sight of him, but all things are naked and laid bare to the eyes of him to whom [we must give our account]" (Heb 4:13). That idea might seem embarrassing to us in light of our pasts, causing us to feel we need to distance ourselves from God. Yet Hebrews 4:13 is actually an invitation to reconcile with God since he has made reconciliation and peace possible through his son (Rom 5:1).

Sin can great a spiritual game of hide and seek. We try to hide things from ourselves, hoping the pain and guilt will dissolve, but we can never hide from God. And we don't need to hide. God seeks us out, desiring to reconcile his relationship with us. We have only to admit our sins and confess our wrongdoings to the one who died for us while we were *still* sinners and enemies of God (Rom 5:8–10). In doing so, we can be found and embraced by the one who was willing to give all on our behalf.

DISCUSSION

A Closer Look

1. The phrases "we reap what we sow" and "what goes around comes around" are common in our culture. How does such a theme work in this story? How does God's grace overturn this idea?

_____

_____

_____

2. Reflect on proper and improper ways we can use our God-given positions of influence and leadership. What is positive about Joseph's leadership? What is negative?

_____

_____

_____

Throughout the Bible

1. Have you ever repaid vengeance with grace and forgiveness? How were your actions received?

_____

_____

_____

2. According to Matthew 18:21-22, how did Joseph's response mirror Christ's teaching?

_____

_____

_____

Beyond the Bible

1. Have you ever experienced hunger like that described in the poem above? How did God provide for your needs? How can you meet others' needs?

_____

_____

_____

2. What is God's greatest act of deliverance in the NT? Can you note any similarities with the Joseph narratives or the exodus?

_____

_____

_____

Application

1. Are there unresolved sins from lingering in your life? What would it take to make this right in your life?

_____

_____

_____

2. Do your feelings of guilt or shame change or alter your view of God? If so, how do you think this influences your trust in him?

_____

_____

_____

CHAPTER 6

TESTING AND FORGIVENESS

Read Genesis 43:1–44:34.

SETTING THE STAGE

Theme. Imagine you are born into a family where you are your father's favorite among 12 children. You enjoy a place of prominence, and you know a rich inheritance awaits you. But your position is not without its downfalls, and when your siblings become overwrought by jealousy, they sell you into slavery and fake your death, telling your father you were brutally killed. Twenty years later, if you were given the perfect opportunity to exact revenge, would you?

When someone violates our sense of justice, we're tempted to seek payback. But Christ's example demonstrated that God requires us to live by radically different principles. Believers should respond as Christ did, by forgiving others instead of seeking to settle the score (see 1 Thess 5:15; Eph 4:32). As Joseph faced the brothers who wronged him, he was in the perfect position to exact revenge. Instead, he exhibited grace, providing us with a pattern for walking in God's image. Yet, as we will see, before Joseph forgave his brothers, he tested them while wrestling with his stormy emotions.

Literary Context. The beginning of Genesis 43–44 resembles that of the previous chapter. The famine continued. Jacob and his sons were once again short on food, having consumed all that the brothers had brought back from Egypt. Jacob again faced the necessity of sending his sons to Egypt to buy grain. There was just one hitch in the plan: Benjamin (Gen 43:1–3).

When his brothers visited Egypt the first time, Joseph sent them home with grain and the order to return with their youngest brother, Benjamin. To ensure their cooperation, he kept one brother, Simeon, in captivity (Gen 42:18–20). When the family ran out of food, it would seem easy enough to simply take Benjamin with them to Egypt and return with both grain and Simeon. But the very thought was impossible for Jacob. When he sent his sons to Egypt the first time, Jacob kept Benjamin behind—he was afraid of losing the only remaining son of his favored wife, Rachel (Gen 42:4; see "Setting the Stage" for Chapter 1). After his remaining sons returned with the news of Simeon's captivity and Joseph's demand that they return with Benjamin, his fears were only heightened, and he initially refused to let them go (Gen 42:38).

But grain from Egypt was their only means of survival, and two of Joseph's brothers tried to coax their father into letting them go by guaranteeing that Benjamin would return. In Genesis 42, Reuben offered up the lives of his own two sons if Benjamin didn't return safely with them (Gen 42:37). Now, to convince their father to allow Benjamin to go with them, Judah also pledged that Benjamin would be safe (Gen 43:8–9). Reuben and Judah had argued against their brothers who wanted to kill Joseph (Gen 37:21–22, 26–27). Here again, they risked themselves by pledging their lives (or, in Reuben's case, the lives of his sons) to guarantee Benjamin's safety.

Historical & Cultural Background. When his brothers returned to Egypt seeking food a second time, Joseph used his position and his brothers' vulnerability to test their character. At one point in his test, Joseph alluded to his power of divination (Gen 44:15), suggesting that these powers gave him knowledge that his brothers had stolen a silver cup from him. While we tend to be highly skeptical of the concept of divination, in the ancient Near East, it was considered a means of gaining information that would otherwise remain unknown.

People used several different methods for divination in the ancient world. In the OT, we frequently read of people casting lots, which was a means of determining God's will or identifying a guilty party (Prov 16:33; Jonah 1:7). In a similar way, some ancients used arrows for divination: The diviner would shoot arrows with markings on them to determine a course of action.[1] Ancient diviners would also examine the liver of a sacrificed animal and read its "signs."[2] Interpreting dreams (seen throughout the Joseph story), consulting the dead (known as necromancy), and observing the stars (astrology) were other popular means of divination.

An additional form of divination, which may be referred to in Joseph's account, involved pouring something—often stones or oil—into water and making interpretations based on the water's reaction. When Joseph's servant mentions his master's use of a silver cup for divination, he may be suggesting that Joseph filled the cup with water for this form of divination (Gen 44:4-6).

Joseph's brothers were already worried about God punishing them for their sin (see Chapter 5). Now, as they faced accusations from someone who claimed to have special knowledge, they had no choice but to admit their guilt (Gen 44:14-16). Of course, Joseph did have more knowledge of their past than they realized—he was the victim of their sin. And through his position of power, Joseph could have easily repaid his brothers for the years of suffering he had endured because of them. But, as we will see, after testing them, he forgave them completely (Gen 45:3-5).

A CLOSER LOOK

By this point, the famine affecting Egypt and the surrounding regions had progressed for two years (see Gen 45:6). Knowing what they faced when they ran out of grain, we can imagine Joseph's brothers tried to stretch the final crumbs they had brought back from Egypt. They had a unique reason for wanting the famine to end. Joseph knew from his dream that his storehouses would need to last for another five years. He also knew that his brothers would soon run out of grain, and he likely expected their return.

Concerned for the survival of his family, Jacob recognized that his sons must return again to Egypt for food (Gen 43:2). But when he instructed them to go, they resisted. Wary of angering the Egyptian official further, they were unwilling to return without Benjamin. Judah spoke for the brothers from this point onward and explained, "The man solemnly admonished us, saying, 'You shall not see my face unless your brother is with you'" (Gen 43:3). Jacob then shifted the blame for this predicament to Judah and the remaining brothers, asking why they had even mentioned Benjamin (Gen 43:6).

The brothers defended themselves: Joseph specifically asked about their father and whether they had other brothers (Gen 43:7). This seems to contradict Genesis 42, which shows the brothers voluntarily offering this unsolicited information in an attempt to convince Joseph of their identity (see especially Gen 42:12–14). The brothers may have been lying to Jacob about the nature of Joseph's inquiry. However, it's more likely that Genesis 42 simply presents a summary of the conversation that took place in Egypt. In fact, Genesis 44:19–20 also references Joseph's specific questioning, making it likely that the earlier account simply excluded this detail.

In a final attempt to placate their father, Judah vowed to be personally responsible for any harm that might come to Benjamin (Gen 43:9). He knew that they had no other option; without additional food from Egypt, all of them—including Benjamin—would die of starvation (Gen 43:8). Judah's response to his father hints at a growing sense of irritation: "If we had not delayed, we would now have returned twice" (Gen 43:10 ESV).

After this back and forth, Jacob reluctantly agreed to let Benjamin go along. To ensure Benjamin's safety, he prepared a gift of the "choice fruits of the land" for the brothers to take to Joseph (Gen 43:11 ESV). But the brothers face an additional dilemma: On the return from their previous journey, they were astonished to discover that the money they had brought for the grain was still in their sacks (Gen 42:28, 35). Surely the Egyptian official—who still held their brother, Simeon—would hold them responsible for this oversight. To prevent this, Jacob instructed his sons to bring twice the original amount (Gen 43:12).

Upon arriving in Egypt, the brothers received an invitation to dine with Joseph in his house (Gen 43:16). They became anxious immediately—an understandable reaction, considering that Joseph had previously accused them of being spies and had imprisoned them for three days. From the thousands of travelers who came to Egypt to buy food, they alone were invited—or sequestered—in Joseph's private residence. They instantly assumed that the Egyptian official would punish them because of the money left in their sacks on their previous visit (Gen 43:18).

Although they could not explain how the money came to be there, the brothers were desperate to exonerate themselves. They didn't wait to be questioned. They preemptively confessed to Joseph's servant how they had found the money on their return trip (Gen 43:19–22). The servant responded encouragingly, stating, "Peace to you; do not be afraid" (Gen 43:23). He then attributed the money to God's work, and released Simeon from prison to join them.

> **Quick Bit:** The Hebrew word *shalom* can mean more than simply "peace." It often refers to a completeness or wholeness, and can also indicate prosperity or something favorable. The term appears several times in Joseph's story. When Jacob asks Joseph to check on his brothers, he literally asks him to "Go, see the peace (*shalom*) of your brothers" (Gen 37:14). When Joseph speaks to his brothers, he asks them about the *shalom* or well-being of their father (Gen 43:27).

When Joseph finally joined them, the brothers again paid homage to him and presented him with the gifts Jacob had sent (Gen 43:26; see also Gen 42:6). Joseph's initial inquiries show his concern for his father. The two years of severe famine could have easily meant death for an elderly person. Aware that Jacob could have passed away since the brothers' previous journey, Joseph first asked if their father, Jacob, was still alive (Gen 43:27). After receiving their reassurances, his focus shifted to Benjamin (Gen 43:29). Upon seeing his only full brother[3] for the first time in more than 20 years, Joseph became overwhelmed with emotion and quickly left the room to weep in private (Gen 43:30).

Joseph soon recovered enough to resume his initial purpose for inviting his brothers to dinner: to test them. The brothers received their first surprise as they sat down for the meal. Dining separately from Joseph (who was served alone due to his status) and the Egyptians (who ate separately because they viewed the Canaanites as inferior),[4] the brothers were shocked to discover that Joseph had seated them exactly according to age (Gen 43:32–33). Since they were grown men, it would have been difficult for an impartial observer to correctly guess their birth order. Joseph, of course, was no impartial observer.

Joseph's next test arrived along with the food. Benjamin, the favored son, was served five times as much food as the other brothers (Gen 43:34). While Joseph may have given Benjamin more food because of his feelings toward his younger brother, he was more likely testing his brothers' reaction. When Joseph held the role of favored son, the brothers reacted to the favoritism by selling him into slavery. Now, Joseph was probably curious whether they would react similarly here.

After the meal, Joseph prepared a final test for his brothers, ordering his silver cup to be hidden in Benjamin's sack (Gen 44:1–2). Again, he designed this ruse to test his brothers' attitudes. Upon discovering the cup in Benjamin's sack, would they turn on their youngest brother to preserve their own lives?

We can imagine the brothers were probably quite relieved the next morning as they prepared to return home. Yet their departure was interrupted by Joseph's servant, who intercepted them and accused them of stealing from Joseph. Oblivious to the cup nestled in Benjamin's food bag, the brothers immediately denied the accusation (Gen 44:6–8). Confident in their innocence, they declared that whoever was found with it should die (Gen 44:9). As if to intentionally draw out the suspense, Joseph's servant searched their sacks, beginning with the oldest. As each successive brother was found to be innocent, their apprehension diminished. The glint of silver that appeared beneath the opening of Benjamin's bag would have likely turned their blood cold (Gen 44:11–12).

The brothers returned to Joseph and fell before him (Gen 44:14), but Joseph did nothing to relieve their fears. He angrily demanded that they account for their actions, implying that his powers of divination alerted him to their theft (Gen 44:15; see "Setting the Stage"). To his surprise, Judah immediately claimed their guilt, despite their innocence regarding the cup (Gen 44:16). Judah may have been simply acknowledging that the cup was found in their sacks, or perhaps he expressing his conviction that God was finally punishing them for selling Joseph as a slave. Either way, Judah's admission of guilt indicates the precariousness of their situation.

The final stage of Joseph's test offered his brothers an easy escape: He would only hold responsible only the individual in whose bag the cup was found; everyone else was free to go. It would have been tempting for the brothers to leave Benjamin and return home. Just as they profited from selling Joseph into slavery (Gen 37:26–28), they could have preserved their lives, taking their money and food to Canaan and leaving Benjamin to live the remainder of his life as a slave to the Egyptian ruler.

Yet the brothers were changed men. Judah—in the longest speech found in Genesis—drew near to Joseph and delivered an impassioned plea explaining Benjamin's importance to their father, Jacob's reluctance to let Benjamin journey to Egypt, and his own pledge to protect Benjamin (Gen 44:18–29). Refusing to act out of self-interest and leave Benjamin behind, Judah's speech proved a change of character on the part of the brothers.

Judah's speech dramatically culminates in his offering to take Benjamin's place (Gen 44:33). He was willing to follow through on his pledge to protect Benjamin, even if it cost him his freedom. As Victor Hamilton notes, "He who once callously engineered the selling of Joseph to strangers out of envy and anger is now willing to become Joseph's slave so that the rest of his brothers, and especially Benjamin, may be freed and allowed to return to Canaan to rejoin their father."[5]

The brothers' response to the test convinced Joseph that they had changed. Years ago when they had sold him into slavery, the brothers had shown no regard for their father's feelings. Now, their father's welfare is their chief concern. This transformation was exactly what Joseph had been hoping for. As the next chapter shows, he becomes overwhelmed with emotion by Judah's words and can no longer conceal his identity from his brothers (Gen 45:1–3).

THROUGHOUT THE BIBLE

Given what we know about Joseph's uprightness, the thought that he would take advantage of his position to test his brothers might cause us to bristle; but tests are a common motif in the OT. They served as a way to distinguish between right and wrong, truth and error. Some tests even served as a means of discerning God's will.

One such test is detailed in Numbers 5: If a jealous husband suspected that his wife had been sexually unfaithful, he could take her to a priest to discover the truth. The woman would be placed before Yahweh while holding a grain offering. The priest would scoop some dust from the floor of the tabernacle and dump it into a jar of holy water. He would then make the woman take an oath:

> If a man has not slept with you, and if you have not had an impurity affair under your husband, go unpunished from the waters of bitterness that brings this curse. But if you have had an affair under your husband, and if you are defiled and a man other than your husband had intercourse with you ... May [God] give you a curse ... in the midst of your people ... making your hip fall away and your stomach swollen; and these waters that bring a curse will go into your intestines to cause your womb to swell and to make your hip fall away." And the women will say, "Amen. Amen" (Num 5:19–22).

The priest would then write the curses down and rinse the ink in the water. Afterward, the woman would drink the water, and her guilt or innocence would be revealed. Although this seems to be a harsh test, it could be beneficial to the wife—if she were innocent, it could protect her from the arbitrary decisions of a jealous husband or judgmental community.

Another test appears in Judges 6. After the Angel of Yahweh commissioned Gideon to deliver Israel from the Midianites (Judg 6:14), Gideon asked for a sign of confirmation to ensure that he was speaking with a divine being (Judg 6:17). He then set a meal before the angel, who touched the food with the tip of his staff. As he did so, "fire went up from the rock and consumed the meat and the unleavened cakes. And the angel of Yahweh went from his sight" (Judg 6:21). Gideon then understood that he had indeed been conversing with the angel of the Yahweh.

Later in the chapter, Gideon again tested God to see if he would deliver Israel by his hand. He set a fleece of wool out at night and said, "If there is dew on the fleece only, and all of the ground is dry, I will know that you will deliver Israel by my hand, just as you have said" (Judg 6:37). God granted his request the following morning (Judg 6:38). Yet just to be sure, Gideon tested God once more, asking, "Do not let your anger burn against me; let me speak once more. Please let me test once more with the fleece; let the fleece be dry, and let there be dew on the ground" (Judg 6:39). Although Scripture warns against putting God to the test (Deut 6:16; Matt 4:7), God was pleased to again satisfy Gideon's request (Judg 6:40).

In addition to these tests, the ancient Israelites had other methods of determining God's will. During his flight from Saul, David called Abiathar the priest to bring the ephod (1 Sam 23:9)—a priestly garment to which the breastpiece was attached. The breastpiece contained two stones called Urim and Thummim, which were used to ascertain God's will. The book of Exodus describes the stones and their function: "And you will put the Urim and Thummim on the breast piece of judgment, and they will be on the heart of Aaron when he comes before Yahweh, and Aaron will bear the judgment of the Israelites on his heart before Yahweh continually" (Exod 28:30). After Abiathar brought the ephod, David asked a series of questions to determine how he should deal with the city of Keilah, which Saul was preparing to besiege (1 Sam 23:10–12). God communicated through the ephod, and both David and Keilah were spared (1 Sam 23:13).

Joseph's tests to determine his brothers' character are simply a fraction of the tests described throughout the OT. While some tests were meant to determine guilt or innocence, others were used to identify people and their motives, and still others were meant to determine God's will. For Joseph, a series of tests enabled him to discern his brothers' character, leading him to show them mercy and forgiveness.

BEYOND THE BIBLE

Joseph endured years of hardship due to his brothers' actions. Despite God's providential involvement, Joseph did not immediately embrace his brothers when they appeared before him in Egypt; he tested them before revealing his identity. The tension and drama of this narrative has inspired reflection on Joseph's story throughout the ages.

> **Quick Bit:** Ephrem the Syrian (ca. 306–373 BC) is best known as a poet and hymn writer. His works are recognized as "the greatest specimens of Christian poetry prior to Dante."[6] He was a widely influential theologian and commentary writer whose works have been adopted across the spectrum of Christian traditions.

Among ancient commentators, Ephrem the Syrian, a fourth-century theologian, reflects artfully on this part of Joseph's ordeal in his *Commentary on Genesis*. Much like commentaries of today, Ephrem was concerned to plumb the depths of the biblical account. His writing displays sensitivity to the tensions that mark Joseph's story. Ephrem captures especially well the sense of anxiety the brothers must have felt before Joseph in Egypt when they received his invitation to dine with them. He writes:

> But when the steward saw how terrified they were, he consoled them and said, "rest assured, do not be afraid. It is not because of the money ... that we are bringing you into the house... You are not going to be condemned... You have been summoned to recline and be seated before our master, for he is just... he wishes to make you forget the disgrace that you endured the first time."[7]

As Ephrem recounts the episode in his commentary, he takes the liberty of speaking on the characters' behalf. This creative interpretation of the characters' interaction would have helped his readers understand the progression and sub-text of events.

Ephrem also captures the emotional turmoil Joseph must have experienced as events progressed. His discussion of Joseph's confrontation with the brothers regarding the silver cup depicts Joseph exploding in full rage.

> Joseph, with the anger of Egyptians, shouted accusations at them and said, *"What is this that you have done?* ... At the great meal that we prepared for you we proclaimed your righteousness among the Egyptians. But today you have become objects of scorn ... because you stole the cup with which I divine for all the Egyptians.[8]

As Genesis 44:16 tells us, Judah responded by confessing to Joseph, "God has found the guilt of your servants!" Here, Ephrem proposes that Judah confessed not only to having stolen the cup, but to the crime he and his brothers committed against Joseph as a young man (an idea Joseph's brothers previously expressed before the Egyptian official; see Gen 42:21–22, 28). Ephrem writes, "Then Judah said, *"Before God the sins of your servants have been discovered"*—not this one [of the cup] but the one for which we have been requited with these things."[9] Ephrem understands Judah's confession within the broader context of God's providential action. Joseph's test was not simply uncovering who "stole" the cup, but the remorse and guilt on the part of the brothers for the crime that initiated the drama playing out before their eyes.

Joseph's tests revealed all that had remained hidden: the changed nature of the brothers, and, as we will see, Joseph's true identity. As the story unfolds, all will see that what was meant for evil, God intended and used for good—a feature of Joseph's account that moved ancient commentators just as it moves us today.

APPLICATION

If anyone had reason for vengeance, it was Joseph. In the many years since his separation from his family, Joseph probably thought about what he might do if he ever met his brothers again. Despite his power, Joseph avoided making rash judgments or abusing his authority. He tested his brothers to see whether they had changed.

As we will see, Joseph ultimately shows compassion to his brothers, fulfilling Jacob's desperate prayer before sending his sons to Egypt for the second time: "May God Almighty grant you mercy before the man" (Gen 43:14 ESV). Despite his immense suffering and the many years he had to dwell on it, Joseph could not bury the fact that these men were his brothers, his family. He knew that acting in retribution would sever those ties forever, and break his father's heart.

Jesus commanded his disciples to live similarly, teaching them to forgive others just as God forgave them (Matt 6:12). In the parable of the Unforgiving Servant (Matt 18:21-35), Jesus spoke of a servant who had a great debt forgiven, but who refused to forgive a man who owed him a small amount; consequently, the servant was harshly punished by his master. Jesus concluded the parable with a severe warning: "So also my heavenly Father will do to every one of you, if you do not forgive your brother from your heart" (Matt 18:35). Jesus makes forgiveness the only option, overturning ancient notions of retribution as well as the ideas of fairness and judgment we carry today.

Ultimately, the choice between vengeance and mercy is a choice between serving ourselves and serving God. Joseph knew that in taking revenge, he would be acting in his own self-interest. By showing mercy, Joseph submitted his will to God's interests and the providential unfolding of his plan, living according to God's ultimate purpose.

DISCUSSION

A Closer Look

1. Have you ever been wronged by someone and later been in a position to treat them the same way? How did you respond?

_____

_____

_____

2. How does Joseph's treatment of his brothers encourage you to respond to those who have treated you unfairly?

_____

_____

_____

Throughout the Bible

1. Can you empathize with Joseph's brothers? Do you think Joseph was right to test them?

_____

_____

_____

2. Have you ever been tested by someone else? Did you feel that it was fair? What did you learn about yourself as a result of it?

_____

_____

_____

Beyond the Bible

1. Have you ever suffered unjustly or had everything taken away from you out of jealousy? Were you, like Joseph, able to see God's hand of providence in your suffering?

_____

_____

_____

2. How might this biblical story be different if Joseph had responded to his brothers in kind? What would be lost?

_____

_____

_____

Application

1. Have you ever struggled with forgiving someone who has done you great harm? What turn of events made you realize whether you forgave them?

_____

_____

_____

2. What prevents you from showing mercy to others when you have the opportunity? Why can it be difficult to show mercy when we so willingly receive it?

_____

_____

_____

CHAPTER 7

SEEING GOD'S PURPOSE

Read Genesis 45:1–47:31.

SETTING THE STAGE

Theme. When circumstances threaten to overwhelm us, we sometimes need an extra measure of grace to do what God calls us to do. Sometimes retrospect can help us recognize the unfolding of God's plan and his use of our actions and the actions of others toward his greater design of growing our faith. Throughout what we perceive as missteps, Scripture tells us that God works out his purpose. And the amazing thing about God's providence is not only that he always works things out according to his plan, but that does so both for our sake and for his glory.

As Joseph revealed his identity to his brothers in Genesis 45, he made it clear that he understood the full picture of God's purpose: The trials and challenges that brought all of them to that moment—from his brothers' jealous actions to Potiphar's wife's lustful attempt to entangle him—all led to his position of power, which preserved his family through famine. Yet if Joseph had chosen revenge instead of forgiveness and restoration, the story could have been very different. God used these apparently unrelated actions to mature Joseph and solidify his faith and ultimately to preserve his people and uphold his promises to Abraham, Isaac, and Jacob (Gen 12:2-3; 15:5-16; 26:3-5; 28:13-15). Although God's ways can be difficult to understand at times, it's clear that he uses everyday events and ordinary people to accomplish his will.

Literary Context. Joseph's story reaches a happy resolution in Genesis 45-47. Despite everything his brothers subjected him to, Joseph ultimately chose not to respond with anger or resentment. Instead, he showed compassion and forgiveness. His recognition that God accomplished his purpose through it all enabled him to let go of the past and not hold it against his brothers (Gen 45:4-8).

This part of Joseph's story recounts the emotional reunion of Jacob and Joseph after 22 years of separation (Gen 46:29-30). Joseph's anticipation in seeing his father again surfaces repeatedly in the account. After revealing his identity to his brothers, Joseph immediately asks about his father's well-being. Jacob, on the other hand, likely hadn't considered the he would ever see his beloved son again; after all, he thought Joseph had fallen victim to a wild animal as a teenager decades earlier (Gen 37:33).[1] Imagine his shock upon learning that not only was Joseph alive, but he was a ruler in Egypt—the same ruler his other sons feared.

Historical & Cultural Background. During his years in Egypt, Joseph developed a knowledge of attitudes and customs unique to Egyptian culture. Genesis 46:34 offers a glimpse of this when Joseph tells his family that "every shepherd is an abomination to the Egyptians" (esv). Despite this, as Joseph's family prepared to move to Egypt, he instructed them to tell Pharaoh that they were shepherds.

Joseph had a clear purpose, though; he wanted his family to live in the land of Goshen, located in the northeastern region of the Nile delta. The fertile Nile delta made Goshen an ideal place to raise livestock. By identifying themselves as shepherds, Joseph's brothers could reasonably suggest Goshen for their settlement. Goshen was also on the geographic margins of Egyptian territory at the time. Given Egyptian disdain for Canaanites, Pharaoh would have wanted to segregate Joseph's family from his Egyptian subjects.[2] Joseph correctly anticipated that Pharaoh would choose the land of Goshen as their settlement (Gen 47:5-6).

We have already seen that the Egyptians had a dismal view of foreigners, especially those from Canaan (see "Setting the Stage," Chapter 5). Yet there is not much evidence in Egyptian literature to substantiate Joseph's statement about the Egyptians' dislike of shepherds. There is a noted absence of shepherds portrayed in ancient Egyptian art, perhaps indicating that they were looked down upon.[3] However, Joseph's statement in Genesis 46:34 most likely reflected a negative attitude toward nomadic people from Egyptians who lived in towns or cities.[4] It may also have reflected their general distrust of foreigners, typically nomadic shepherds. Regardless, Joseph's instructions to his family paid off; Pharaoh gave them the land of Goshen, just as Joseph had hoped.

A CLOSER LOOK

As Genesis 45 opens, we know that Joseph's tests have finally produced the results he desired. Judah's impassioned speech confirmed for Joseph that his brothers were changed men (see Gen 44:18-34). Joseph could no longer contain his emotions as Judah described the heartbreak that would befall his father should Benjamin be taken from him (Gen 45:1). Having witnessed their change of heart and Judah's willingness to trade his life for Benjamin, Joseph wept as he finally told them who he was (Gen 45:2-3).

The brothers, stunned into silence, were shocked by Joseph's revelation (Gen 45:3). In an instant, they were confronted with the unbelievable truth that Joseph—the brother they sold into slavery—was alive and now second in command in Egypt. The revelation terrified them. What would he do? Would he exact revenge? Would he have them killed?

Joseph reassured them, saying, "Do not be distressed and do not be angry with yourselves that you sold me here, for God sent me as deliverance before you" (Gen 45:5). He immediately calmed their fears, proclaiming that *God* had sent him to Egypt:

> And God sent me before you all to preserve for you a remnant in the land and to keep alive among you many survivors. So now, you yourselves did not send me here, but God put me here as father to Pharaoh and as master of all his household, and a ruler over all the land of Egypt (Gen 45:7-8).

Joseph's thoughts then immediately turned to his father. It was Judah's plea for Jacob that brought Joseph to the point of emotional breakdown (see Gen 44:18-34). He instructed his brothers to bring Jacob to Egypt along with the rest of the family. With five more years of famine to endure,

Joseph wanted to ensure that his family was provided for. He commanded them, "And you must tell my father of all my honor in Egypt and all that you have seen. Now hurry and bring my father here" (Gen 45:13).

He then turned his attention to Benjamin—his only full brother—and then embraced each of his brothers in turn as he cried with them (Gen 45:14–15). Word of their tearful reunion made its way back to Pharaoh, who was pleased with the news that Joseph's brothers had come to Egypt (Gen 45:16). He summoned Joseph and gave him instructions concerning his family: "Take your father and your households and come to me, and I will give you the best of the land of Egypt, and you shall eat the fat of the land" (Gen 45:18). Demonstrating his high regard for Joseph, Pharaoh provided the brothers with wagons and food for their journey home and back. He also conveyed that they need not worry about bringing their possessions when they returned—he would give them the best Egypt had to offer (Gen 45:20).

Joseph also showed generosity to his brothers, giving them additional provisions (Gen 45:21). He did not distribute the gifts equally, however, as he lavished Benjamin with 300 pieces of silver and five changes of clothes (Gen 45:22). He likewise sent extravagant gifts and provisions for his father (Gen 45:23)—evidence that he was alive and held a high position in Egypt. As the brothers departed, Joseph instructed them not to quarrel, probably meaning that he did not want them to place blame for sins committed long ago.

We can imagine the brothers' astonishment as they traveled back to Canaan to report all these things to their father (Gen 45:25–26). Jacob was understandably stunned by the news—so shocked, in fact, that at first he didn't believe them (Gen 45:26). But he couldn't ignore Joseph's message and the presence of the wagons and gifts, and he eventually realized that his sons weren't lying. He agreed to go, stating, "It is enough. Joseph my son is still alive. I will go and see him before I die" (Gen 45:28). With his sons, Jacob began the journey to Egypt to see the son he thought was dead.

En route to Egypt, Jacob paused at Beersheba, the southernmost portion of Palestine, to offer sacrifices to God—a location of enduring significance for him and his ancestors. It was there that Abraham called on the name of Yahweh and settled his family (Gen 21:33–34; 22:19). It was there that Abraham's son, Isaac (Jacob's father), was added to the Abrahamic covenant (Gen 26:23–25). Isaac built an altar in Beersheba to God in response to his blessing—presumably the same one his son Jacob used when he stopped there (Gen 46:1).

The text never explains why Jacob stopped at Beersheba. He may have been apprehensive about leaving the promised land, or he may have recalled God's pronouncement to Abraham in Genesis 15:13.[5] Jacob may have recalled that God had explicitly forbidden his father, Isaac, from seeking refuge in Egypt during a famine: "And Yahweh appeared to [Isaac] and said, 'Do not go down to Egypt; dwell in the land which I will show to you'" (Gen 26:2). God emphatically declared that he would make Isaac a great nation *within Canaan*, not outside of it (Gen 26:3–5).

Whatever the reason for his stopping, Jacob encountered the divine at Beersheba, just as his father and grandfather had. God appeared to Jacob and reassured him of his present journey (Gen 46:2). He told Jacob that he would extend the promises of the Abrahamic covenant to him and make him a great nation *while in Egypt*: "I am the God, the God of your father. Do not be afraid to go down to Egypt, for I will make you a great nation there" (Gen 46:3). He also told Jacob that he would die in Egypt in Joseph's presence, and that he would one day bring him from Egypt (Gen 46:4). God tenderly eased Jacob's fears, showing him that the journey to Egypt was part of his plan. With this reassurance, Jacob resumed his travels.

When Jacob and his family arrived in Goshen, Joseph hurried to meet them. Seeing his father, Joseph "presented himself to him and fell upon his neck and wept upon his neck a long time" (Gen 46:29). Following their emotional reunion, Joseph prepared the family for their forthcoming audience with Pharaoh (Gen 46:31–34; see "Setting the Stage").

Joseph selected five of his brothers and took them before Pharaoh, who asked them of their occupation (Gen 47:1–3). Although the brothers knew that the Egyptians loathed shepherds, they answered him honestly, just as Joseph had instructed them (see Gen 46:34). Any apprehension they might have had disappeared as Pharaoh granted them the territory of Goshen with its fertile lands to pasture their flocks. Pharaoh also instructed Joseph to put his livestock in their care—further evidence of Pharaoh's high regard for him (Gen 47:5–6). Joseph then brought his father, Jacob, before Pharaoh, and Jacob blessed him (Gen 47:7–10). This part of the narrative ends with a summary that indicates Joseph's purpose in being brought to Egypt: "And Joseph provided his father and his brothers and all the household of his father with food, according to the number of their children" (Gen 47:12).

The story then turns from Joseph's interaction with his family to his dealings with the Egyptians (Gen 47:13–26). As the famine intensified, the Egyptians approached Joseph to buy more food. As time passed, they ran out of means for purchasing grain. After their money was depleted, they returned the next year and gave up their livestock for food. The following year they sold their land and then themselves as slaves to Pharaoh. By the time the famine was over, Pharaoh owned everything in Egypt except the holdings of the government-sponsored priests. This part of the story serves to contrast Joseph's benevolence to his family with his shrewd administration over the Egyptian population.

> **Quick Bit:** The language used to describe Joseph's family in Genesis 47:27 is also used for the Israelites in Exodus 1:7. The "fruitfulness" of the Israelites in Egypt eventually causes Pharaoh to turn on them, culminating in the exodus. With this language, the biblical narrative ties together the experience of Joseph's family and the deliverance of Israel in the exodus, God's most powerful display of salvation in the OT.

Despite the difficult circumstances, Joseph's family prospered and multiplied greatly in Goshen (Gen 47:27)—continuing evidence of God's promise to remain faithful to his covenant (see Gen 46:3). Joseph and Jacob enjoyed 17 years together in Goshen before Jacob sensed that his time to die had come (Gen 47:28–29). Before blessing his sons, he called Joseph to him and made him swear to carry his body back to Canaan, the land of his ancestors (Gen 47:29–31)—an oath that Joseph fulfills in Genesis 50:1–14. The two seal their oath in typical ancient Near Eastern fashion: with one person placing his hand under the other's thigh—a euphemistic way of describing one male grasping the genitals of another. In antiquity, the male reproductive organs were viewed as sacred objects and were often invoked in oath making. The story then transitions into Jacob's final blessing of his sons in Genesis 48–49.

Through this long-awaited reunion, we see how God had woven the strands of their lives into a masterpiece. Through all of Joseph's trials—his abandonment in the well, his time of servitude, the false charges against, him, his time in prison—God protected him and sustained his family. Now, God had also restored his family's standing and repaired their broken relationships. They could all put the sins and sorrows of the past behind them and rejoice in their new life together. God's divine use of their circumstances testifies to his sovereignty and reflects his covenant loyalty: through it all, God remained true to his original promises to Abraham, Joseph's ancestor (Gen 12:2–3).

THROUGHOUT THE BIBLE

Joseph's speech to his brothers in Genesis 45 reveals his confidence in God's sovereignty. Although unsure of the details up to that point, he was aware that God was working in and through him to accomplish a greater purpose. He came to realize that God had chosen him to be a channel of salvation for his family and the whole world (Gen 41:57). But Joseph's story was merely one act in God's redemptive work. Something even bigger was taking place behind the scenes.

In Genesis 12 (and several times thereafter), God promised Abraham that he would become a great nation and that all the nations of the world would be blessed through him (Gen 12:2–3). Part of his covenant faithfulness to Abraham included ensuring the welfare of his family; without them, Abraham would have no legacy. But God also told Abraham that his descendants would spend roughly 400 years in a foreign land. He delivered this news with a glimpse of hope: "Know this for certain, that your offspring shall be aliens in a land that is not theirs, and shall be slaves there, and they shall be oppressed for four hundred years; but I will bring judgment on the nation that they serve, and afterward they shall come out with great possessions" (Gen 15:13–14 NRSV).

Egypt was the nation God referred to, and Joseph was the means by which God led Israel there. As we've seen, he did so to sustain Joseph's (and Abraham's) family despite a devastating famine. But in addition to keeping his word to Abraham and preserving his descendants, God was setting the stage for his greatest act of redemption prior to sending his Son: the exodus from Egypt, the event referred to in Genesis 15:14.

Long after Joseph died and the memory of his provision for God's people faded, Egypt turned on Israel. Exodus 1:6–7 gives the background: "Then Joseph died, and all his brothers, and that whole generation. But the Israelites were fruitful and prolific; they multiplied and grew exceedingly strong, so that the land was filled with them" (NRSV). The next verse foreshadows their impending slavery: "Now a new king arose over Egypt, who did not know Joseph" (Exod 1:8 NRSV). Israel had strength in numbers, and the new Pharaoh feared a revolt. As a result, he forced Israel into slavery (Exod 1:10–14).

As the story unfolds, God fulfills the word he declared to Abraham in Genesis 15. He works mightily to deliver Israel from bondage in Egypt, and the exodus becomes a landmark in Israelite history. The imagery of the exodus account becomes synonymous with God's deliverance throughout the Bible (Deut 20:1; Josh 24:17; Jude 5). In times of distress and oppression, God's people look to the exodus and recall the unparalleled redemptive power of the Creator. And when Jesus—through whom God brings about his ultimate act of salvation—arrives on the scene, many events in his life parallel events from the exodus (Matt 2:15; compare Exod 1:22 and Matt 2:16).

God worked through Joseph to bring about great salvation. But God also used Joseph to bring his people to Egypt so that he could display his redemptive power through the exodus, an event that would become the penultimate example of God's power and deliverance.

BEYOND THE BIBLE

Joseph needed an abundance of grace to respond the way he did—and God gave it to him. Seeing his brothers for the first time after many years evoked a flood of emotions. Revealing his identity to them and witnessing their shock no doubt forced him to recollect the suffering he had endured before rising to his place of prominence. But Joseph had come to understand God's hand in his experiences. So rather than bitterly recall the past, Joseph hopefully embraced the future. God had extended his grace to Joseph, and now it was Joseph's chance to do the same for his family.

His response was counterintuitive; most of us would have exacted vengeance. Despite the wrong he suffered, he loved those who wronged him because he recognized God's sovereignty over his situation (Gen 45:4–8; 50:20). *The Testament of Joseph*, a document from the second century BC, describes the paradox of Joseph's life:

> In my life I have seen envy and death.
> But I have not gone astray: I continued in the truth of the Lord.
> These, my brothers, hated me but the Lord loved me.
> They wanted to kill me, but the God of my fathers preserved me.
> Into a cistern they lowered me; the Most High raised me up.
> They sold me into slavery; the Lord of all set me free.
> I was taken into captivity; the strength of his hand came to my aid.
> I was overtaken by hunger; the Lord himself fed me generously.
> I was alone, and God came to help me.
> I was in weakness, and the Lord showed his concern for me.
> I was in prison, and the Savior acted graciously in my behalf.
> I was in bonds, and he loosed me;
> falsely accused, and he testified in my behalf.
> Assaulted by bitter words of the Egyptians, and he rescued me.
> A slave, and he exalted me.[6]

Quick Bit: *The Testament of Joseph* is part of a larger work, *The Testaments of the Twelve Patriarchs*—a collection of writings that dates to approximately the second century BC and purports to be the final words of Jacob's 12 sons. These works belong to the Old Testament Pseudepigrapha, a body of literature supposedly written by significant people from Israelite history, such as Moses and Enoch. Although these texts were written centuries after these people died, ascribing authorship to them lent credence and authority to the writings. This was a common and accepted literary form in Israel's Second Temple period (ca. 515 BC–AD 73).

Recognizing God's greater purpose behind his trials allowed Joseph to let go of whatever bitterness he may have experienced, enabling him to forgive his brothers. He felt no grudge, but instead loved his brothers despite their sin against him. He resolved to embrace his role, care for his family, and display the same love and grace that God had showed him. *The Testament of Joseph* also communicates this point, depicting Joseph speaking these words:

> After the death of Jacob, my father, I loved them beyond measure, and everything he had wanted for them I did abundantly on their behalf. I did not permit them to be troubled by the slightest matter, and everything I had under my control I gave to them. Their sons were mine, and mine were as their servants; their life was as my life, and every pain of theirs was my pain; every ailment of theirs was my sickness; their wish was my wish. I did not exalt myself above them arrogantly because of my worldly position of glory, but I was among them as one of the least.[7]

Joseph's attitude not only reflected God's, but it paralleled Jesus' response to sinful humanity almost 1,500 years later. Joseph chose to love and care for those who wronged him even though they deserved punishment. His character serves as a model of faithfulness, virtue, and wisdom. It also encourages us to see our life and our own trials as God sees them: as opportunities for personal growth as well as the means by which he forms us as disciples.

APPLICATION

We often struggle to recognize how difficult circumstances can be used for good—especially when they disrupt our own lives. Even though Scripture tells us to "rejoice in our afflictions" (Rom 5:3 ESV), this is much easier said than done. Yet, as Joseph's story demonstrates, God can use the most trying of circumstances and the most unlikely people to accomplish his purpose.

Joseph understood that God was using his own trials for good—not just in his own life, but also for the sake of his family (Gen 45:4–8). His story shows us that he had this perspective from the beginning. As a servant in Potiphar's house, he remained aware of God's presence in his life, refusing to sin in succumbing to Potiphar's wife (Gen 39:9). During his imprisonment, he used his God-given ability to help others, anticipating that it might one day secure his release from prison (Gen 40:14).

In Genesis 45:4-8, Joseph makes explicit what he has already discerned: that God had providentially orchestrated the events of his life to serve a greater purpose.

In his first letter to the Corinthians, Paul reflects a similar view: "But God chose what is foolish in the world to shame the wise; God chose what is weak in the world to shame the strong; God chose what is low and despised in the world, even things that are not, to bring to nothing things that are" (1 Cor 1:27-28 ESV). Paul himself was living proof of this truth. Having persecuted "the church of God" (1 Cor 15:9), Paul was the least likely candidate for spreading the gospel throughout the world. But God saw fit to call him to take the gospel to the Gentiles. In fact, Paul says that God had selected him for this task even *before* he was born (Gal 1:15). Although God knew Paul would one day try to "destroy" the church (Gal 1:13), he was "pleased" to use Paul to bring the gospel to the nations (Gal 1:16).

The Bible testifies to how God can use the "foolish" things of the world to accomplish his will. Sustained by his fervent trust in God, Joseph eventually came to understand God's ultimate purpose.

DISCUSSION

A Closer Look

1. How might things have been different for Joseph and his family had he chosen to respond vengefully? What effect would this have had on Israel's history?

_____

_____

_____

2. Do you think Joseph was wrong to allow the Egyptians to sell everything while he provided for his family? Why or why not?

_____

_____

_____

Throughout the Bible

1. Do you have landmark events in your life that cause you to reflect on God's power and deliverance? What are they?

_____

_____

_____

2. Can you think of other ways in which Jesus' life mirrors the exodus or its central figure, Moses?

_____

_____

_____

Beyond the Bible

1. Can you think of a time in your life when God showed profound grace in your life? Did this motivate you to be gracious to others?

_____

_____

_____

2. Have you ever wronged someone only to have them forgive and embrace you in return? What effect did this have on you? How did you see Christ in that response?

_____

_____

_____

Application

1. Identify a negative or trying event from your past that God used for his good. How did you sustain a sense of God's presence throughout that time?

_____

_____

_____

2. How can you cultivate a healthy awareness of God's work in your life? What causes you to doubt God's presence?

_____

_____

_____

CHAPTER 8

FINDING FORGIVENESS

Read Genesis 48:1–50:26.

SETTING THE STAGE

Theme. Although people long for happy endings, we sometimes forget that reconciliation always demands a reckoning. When you truly forgive someone, you acknowledge that you have been wronged, and you agree to bear the cost yourself. Our model for forgiveness, of course, is God himself. The struggle and pain of a broken and sinful world will be made right when God restores his creation (Rev 21:1–7), but that resolution comes at a tremendous cost—the life of his Son.

Our assurance of forgiveness and restoration through Christ contrasts starkly with the uncertainty experienced by Joseph's brothers. After Jacob died, Joseph's brothers once again feared that Joseph would make them pay for their past sins. If he had continued to hold a grudge, he now had the perfect opportunity to avenge himself. Instead, Joseph forgave his brothers even more deeply than before. His willingness to pardon them, despite the struggles he endured for so long, provides a model for our own journey through painful circumstances to a future when God will make "all things new" (Rev 21:5).

Literary Context. By the end of Genesis 47, all the major conflicts in the story of Joseph have been resolved. The famine has ended. Joseph has been reunited with his brothers and his father. Jacob has given Joseph final instructions to bury him in his homeland in Canaan (Gen 47:29–31).

Joseph's story, however, is part of a larger story—the story of Abraham's descendants and God's plan to redeem the world.

Genesis 48–50 provides a fitting conclusion to the life of Jacob and his 12 sons. Just as Isaac blessed Jacob instead of Esau (Gen 27:18–40), Jacob now blesses Ephraim over Manasseh (Gen 48:14–19). Jacob's final words to each of his sons summarizes their past actions (Gen 49:4, 5–6) and points to the future of Israel (the "twelve tribes of Israel" in Gen 49:28). The book of Genesis ends with Joseph's death. With all the sons of Israel living in Egypt, this conclusion sets the stage for the events of Exodus to unfold (see "Throughout the Bible," Chapter 7). Joseph's words before his death, "God will certainly visit you and bring you up from this land to the land that he swore to Abraham, to Isaac, and to Jacob" (Gen 50:24), point to this next chapter of Israel's story—God's deliverance of the Israelites from Egypt.

Exodus 1 continues where Genesis 50 leaves off. It begins by recounting the death of Joseph (Exod 1:6; compare Gen 50:26), then leaps forward to the time of Israel's slavery in Egypt. The narrative describes both the surge in the Israelite population and the transition of power in Egypt to a ruler who did not know Joseph (Exod 1:7–8). It also quotes Joseph's dying request: that the sons of Israel swear to take his bones out of Egypt with them (Exod 13:19; compare Gen 50:25).

Historical & Cultural Background. When Jacob and Joseph died, the text notes that the physicians of Egypt embalmed their bodies (Gen 50:2–3, 26). The ancient Egyptians invented the process of embalming, or mummification, to preserve corpses for long periods. They believed that this process created a physical dwelling for the soul of the deceased.[1]

Mummification involved several steps. First embalmers washed the corpse with water and spiced wine. Then they removed the internal organs (liver, lungs, stomach, intestines, and brain) and dried them in natron, a combination of salt, sodium carbonate, and sodium bicarbonate. They also stuffed and covered the body with natron. After about 40 days, the body would be completely dehydrated.

The embalmers then washed the body again and oiled the skin. They wrapped the internal organs in linen and either returned them to the body or placed them in canopic jars—stone or clay jars often carved with the heads of the four sons of the Egyptian deity, Horus—which would be buried next to the body. Finally, the body would be wrapped with several layers of linen bandages bonded with resin.

Funerals were held after the entire mummification process was complete. The 70 days of mourning for Jacob mentioned in Genesis 50:3 included the 40 days of embalming as well as the typical 30 days of mourning (see Num 20:29; Deut 34:8). Although mummification was associated with Egyptian religious practices, neither Jacob nor Joseph were buried in an Egyptian tomb. Both were later buried in the promised land of Canaan (Gen 50:4-14; Josh 24:32).

A CLOSER LOOK

Despite the hardship Joseph endured, God worked through every circumstance to further his purpose. He positioned Joseph to save thousands of lives by promoting him to the heights of Egyptian government. He cared for Joseph's relatives—Abraham's descendants—according to his covenant in Genesis 12:2-3. He reunited and healed Joseph's fractured family. He provided a haven of rest and abundance so that the young nation of Israel could survive and grow, even in desperate times.

But more heartache loomed on the horizon: Jacob was dying. Joseph had dedicated 17 years to caring for his elderly father (Gen 47:28) and restoring the father-son affection the two previously enjoyed. When that season came to an end, Joseph's actions in Genesis 48 and 50 portray the depth of his grief.

When he learned of his father's condition, Joseph immediately took his two sons to see their grandfather (Gen 48:1). When they arrived, Jacob summoned his strength and sat up in bed (Gen 48:2). As was customary in the ancient world, fathers imparted blessings to their children and grandchildren before dying, and Jacob welcomed this role. He began by reiterating God's covenant with Abraham and his descendants and the promise of a divine inheritance in Israel (Gen 48:3-4; compare Gen 35:9-15). Then he formally adopted Joseph's sons so that they would have a share in the promised land (Gen 48:5).

Jacob then blessed both of Joseph's sons, but in reverse order, giving the younger son the blessing of the older (Gen 48:14-16). This troubled Joseph (Gen 48:17-18), but Jacob spoke prophetically saying, "'I know, my son; I know. [The older] also shall become a people, and he also shall be great, but his younger brother shall be greater than him, and his offspring shall become a multitude of nations'" (Gen 48:19). This role reversal echoes the blessings of Jacob and Esau (Gen 27:18-40); it also parallels Jacob's favoritism of Joseph over his older brothers (Gen 37:2-4).

After blessing Joseph's sons, Jacob blessed Joseph and gave him a greater portion than the rest of his brothers (Gen 48:21-22). After meeting with Joseph and his sons privately, Jacob called all of his sons to himself. But not all of them would receive his blessing. His first three sons—Reuben, Simeon, and Levi—incurred harsh rebukes and curses (Gen 49:3-7). Judah, next after Levi, was given the right to rule within the family with the promise that a king would come from his tribe (Gen 49:8-12; see "Throughout the Bible"). The other brothers received blessings that reflected their destiny in Israel's history (Gen 49:13-21), but Joseph was given an extra benediction (Gen 49:22-26).

In the first part of Joseph's blessing, Jacob recognizes his success in the face of hostility. After describing Joseph's prosperity, Jacob said, "The archers fiercely attacked him; they shot at him and pressed him hard" (Gen 49:23 NRSV). Throughout his life, Joseph had been attacked by opponents, particularly his brothers and Potiphar's wife. But sustained by God, he overcame all these obstacles (Gen 49:24-25).

As the blessing continued, Jacob shifted to Joseph's future: "the Almighty ... will bless you with blessings of heaven above, blessings of the deep that lies beneath, blessings of the breasts and of the womb" (Gen 49:25 NRSV). Jacob affirmed his confidence in God's continued assistance in Joseph's life, noting that it would be characterized by provision, abundance, and fertility.

Jacob assured Joseph that his words were binding: "The blessings of your father are stronger than the blessings of the eternal mountains" (Gen 49:26 NRSV). He further distinguished Joseph over his brothers: "May [these blessings] be on the head of Joseph, and on the forehead of the prince of his brothers" (Gen 49:26). The firstborn son of Jacob's favorite wife now received honor and blessing for saving his family and for demonstrating integrity and righteousness despite opposition and hardship.

After his final words to his sons, Jacob asked to be buried at the family gravesite at Machpelah (Gen 49:29-32), which Abraham purchased in Genesis 23. When Jacob died (Gen 49:33), Joseph grieved more visibly than his brothers: "Joseph fell on his father's face and wept upon him and kissed him" (Gen 50:1). He ordered that Jacob be embalmed according to Egyptian custom, and he led a massive funerary procession to Machpelah to bury his father (Gen 50:2-14).

Grief wasn't the only emotion Jacob's death ignited. With their father's passing, Joseph's brothers began to fear once again that Joseph would take vengeance for their evil past (Gen 50:15). Jacob had been a restraining force; Joseph loved his father too much to bring him more heartache. But now, with Jacob gone, the brothers worried that Joseph no longer had to concern himself with their father.

The brothers approached Joseph with a plea. They claimed that before their father died, he asked Joseph to pardon their sin (Gen 50:16-17). The Bible doesn't record whether such an exchange ever took place between Jacob and his sons. In light of their fear and guilt, their story seems contrived. Awash in worry, they likely forgot that Joseph had already pardoned them and expressed his confidence in God's sovereignty (see Gen 45:5-8).

Joseph defied their expectations. Weeping, he reassured them that he had no harmful intentions against them, and he confidently asserted his understanding of the family's turbulent history and God's sovereign design: "As for you, you planned evil against me, but God planned it for good, in order to do this—to keep many people alive—as it is today" (Gen 50:20). With these words Joseph calmed their fears and acknowledged his life's purpose.

As the Joseph narrative concludes, Israel's prophetic blessing of his sons and grandsons comes to pass just as he said. Joseph lived 110 years, the ideal life span in Egyptian culture (Gen 50:22). He also lived to see his great-grandchildren (Gen 50:23). Shortly before he died, he foretold Israel's exodus from Egypt and commanded that his bones be taken with them (Gen 50:24-25)—a command fulfilled in Exodus 13:19 and Joshua 24:32. When Joseph breathed his last, he could do so in peace (Gen 50:26). He persevered and held fast to his faith despite crushing adversity, and went on to be used by God to provide for his family, a nation, and the world. Joseph's death marked the closing strains of one of God's greatest orchestrations and paved the way for God's purpose to advance.

THROUGHOUT THE BIBLE

Among the many benefits that arose from Joseph's trials, Jacob's blessing of Judah ranks near the top (Gen 49:8-12). On his deathbed in Egypt, Jacob spoke honestly and prophetically about his sons. His words to Judah have a tremendous bearing on the most important redemption story in history: the coming of the Messiah.

Jacob's first three sons' bad behavior earned them harsh rebukes. Reuben seduced Bilhah, his father's concubine (Gen 35:22), a shameful act that brought him Jacob's censure (Gen 49:3-4). Simeon and Levi, Jacob's second and third sons, orchestrated the slaughter at Shechem (Gen 34:25-31) to avenge their sister's rape; they, too, received their father's curse (Gen 49:5-7). So Judah, fourth in line, inherited his father's blessing.

Jacob described Judah's future as a leader among his brothers: "The sons of your father shall bow down to you" (Gen 49:8). He granted Judah a position of authority among his descendants: "The scepter shall not depart from Judah, nor the ruler's staff from between his feet, until tribute comes to him; and the obedience of the peoples is his" (Gen 49:10 NRSV). Genesis 49:11-12 describes the abundance of the land that Judah would one day inherit.

Centuries later, when Israel settled the promised land, the nation asked for a ruler to lead them in battle (Deut 17:14-15; 1 Sam 8:5, 20). After Saul failed as king, God raised David—a descendant of Judah—to lead the nation (Gen 38:27-30; Ruth 4:18-22). God later made a covenant with David and promised to establish his throne forever (2 Sam 7). This promise pointed to the Messiah—the savior and deliverer of Israel, a descendant of David and Judah.

The Gospels depict Jesus as the fulfillment of the promise originally spoken to Judah. Matthew 1:2-6 establishes Jesus' relationship to the line of Judah and David, as does Luke 3:31-34. The Gospels repeatedly refer to Jesus as the "Son of David" (Matt 9:27; 12:23; 21:9; 22:42). The image of the ferocious lion described by Jacob in Genesis 49:8-9 came to be associated with the Messiah. Revelation 5:5 affirms Jesus' heritage in the figures of Judah and David: "Do not weep! Behold, the lion of the tribe of Judah, the root of David, has conquered, so that he can open the scroll and its seven seals."

Joseph's story is not simply about God's redemptive use of suffering for a single family; it reflects the larger story of redemption told throughout the biblical narrative. The blessing that Jacob bestowed on Judah established his descendants as the future rulers of Israel, which in turn supported David's later claim to the throne. Not only had God commanded his prophet Samuel to anoint David, but Jacob had prophesied centuries earlier that a descendant of Judah would rule Israel. And from this kingly line came Jesus, the Messiah, who will establish his throne when he returns (Rev 20:4; 22:1-5).

BEYOND THE BIBLE

In addition to passages such as Genesis 49:8-12, texts beyond the Bible also discuss messianic expectations. Several Jewish texts from various traditions describe the Messiah's coming. Although some sources are more specific than others, most emphasize a connection to King David, a descendant of Judah.

> **Quick Bit:** The term "messianic expectations" describes the various views about the Messiah during a given period of Israel's history. Jews expected the Messiah to come, but they had different ideas about what he would be like. Some anticipated a priestly figure, while others looked for a military leader who would defeat Israel's enemies. Some "messianic expectations" combined these two ideals.

Among these texts is a document from the Dead Sea Scrolls called 4Q252 (from Cave 4 at Qumran, fragment number 252). This fragment is part of a collection of documents thought to be a commentary on the book of

Genesis. The text, probably dating from the first century BC, was written by the *Yahad*—a Hebrew term meaning "community" that refers to the group that wrote some of the scrolls and possibly lived at Qumran. Scroll 4Q252 outlines some of their messianic expectations:

> [...] a ruler shall [no]t depart from the tribe of Judah while Israel has dominion. [And] the one who sits on the throne of David [shall never] be cut off, because the "ruler's staff" is the covenant of the kingdom, [and the thous]ands of Israel are "the feet," until the Righteous Messiah, the Branch of David, has come. For to him and to his seed the covenant of the kingdom of his people has been given for the eternal generations, because he has kept [...] the Law with the men of the *Yahad*.[2]

This text was written before the birth of Jesus, but it is consistent with the messianic expectations of the day. The community at Qumran (the *Yahad*) understood that the Messiah must come from Judah, that he would descend from David, and that he would rule forever on David's throne (2 Sam 7).

Quick Bit: The Dead Sea Scrolls were discovered in 1947 along the shores of the Dead Sea in a series of caves. They contain both biblical and nonbiblical manuscripts. The biblical manuscripts include all the books of the OT except Esther and date to roughly the first and second centuries BC.

As a commentary on Genesis, the scrolls' understanding of the Messiah drew from Jacob's prophecy in Genesis 49:8–12 ("a ruler shall not depart from the tribe of Judah," "ruler's staff," "feet"). The Qumran community lived more than 1,000 years after Jacob's prophecy and was heavily influenced by God's promise to David in 2 Samuel 7. They looked across the Hebrew Bible, identified the passages thought to refer to the Messiah, and developed a picture of what his character would be like. Although their understanding varies from scroll to scroll, the picture in 4Q252 is consistent with what we know of the time period and from the OT. About a century later, Jesus fulfilled these OT messianic expectations, which were themselves shaped by Joseph's experiences in Genesis 37–50.

APPLICATION

The highs and lows of Joseph's story bring him back to where he began: with his father and his brothers. Beginning with Joseph's dreams and the subsequent treachery of his brothers (Gen 37), the narrative closes with Joseph's brothers unable to trust him, even though he had already forgiven them. They try to establish a "truce" by concocting a story about their father (Gen 50:15-17) and then by offering to become his slaves (50:18). In doing so, Joseph's brothers fulfilled the very dreams that had prompted them to betray him in the first place.

Joseph's brothers were crippled by guilt. Their inability to accept his forgiveness resonates within many Christians. Like Joseph's brothers, we have been offered extraordinary forgiveness, but we often fail to let it permeate our lives. Instead of accepting God's unrestricted forgiveness in Christ, we may try to secure forgiveness for ourselves rather than depend on the only source of hope and peace: the death and resurrection of Christ.

Christians celebrate the Lord's Supper (or the Eucharist) to remember what Christ accomplished on our behalf. According to Matthew's Gospel, Jesus presented the cup to his disciples during his final meal and spoke the following words: "This is my blood of the covenant which is poured out for many for the forgiveness of sins" (Matt 26:28). When Paul wrote to the Corinthians, he told them to celebrate the meal as a way of proclaiming the Lord's death (1 Cor 11:23-26). Paul knew that by recalling the significance of the work of Christ, the Corinthians would grow to trust God's saving grace more and more.

As believers in Christ, we are invited to place our full trust in God's promise to deliver us from the bondage of sin. Even Joseph's generous offer to forgive his brothers pales in comparison. Although we may struggle to accept this deep truth, God offers us full reassurance of our standing before him. As Paul proclaims in Romans, there is *nothing* that can separate us from "the love of God that is in Christ Jesus our Lord" (Rom 8:38). And this is the great hope of the Christian life: We have a God who will sustain us through life's difficulties until our salvation is fully realized (Rev 21:1-7).

DISCUSSION

A Closer Look

1. Can you think of a time when you were able to detect God's goodness in the midst of your trials?

_____

_____

_____

2. How has God used your trials for the benefit of others? How have you grown as a result of them?

_____

_____

_____

Throughout the Bible

1. What other good things came out of Joseph's situation? Can you identify some lasting benefits?

_____

_____

_____

2. Perez, the son of Judah by his daughter-in-law (Gen 38), is included in Jesus' genealogy, along with other characters with shameful origins. What does this communicate about Jesus' mission? How does it give you hope?

_____

_____

_____

Beyond the Bible

1. Can you think of other texts from the OT that describe the Messiah? How does Jesus fulfill these expectations?

_____

_____

_____

2. Certain expectations surround Jesus' second coming, just as they did his first. Can you name some of them?

_____

_____

_____

Application

1. We often meet God's remarkable offer of forgiveness with open arms. What causes you to question this reality as life progresses? What helps you accept God's forgiveness?

_____

_____

_____

2. The Lord's Supper is a powerful gift from God to the Church for remembering the saving work of Christ. What other practices help us recall Christ's work?

_____

_____

_____

CONCLUSION

Joseph provides a nearly flawless model for faithful living. Throughout the various trials he experienced, he remained devoted to God. As a slave, he rejected the temptations of his master's wife, steadfastly refusing to "sin against God" or his master (Gen 39:9). When his faithfulness resulted in wrongful imprisonment, he continued to demonstrate his trust in God by telling the chief baker and cupbearer that "interpretations belong to God" (Gen 40:8). When he was eventually brought before Pharaoh, Joseph pointed not to his own abilities, but to God's power (Gen 41:16).

Joseph also remained faithful when he was prosperous. He attributed his rise to power to God's doing, naming his son Ephraim to declare that it was God who made him fruitful (Gen 41:52). When he was finally reunited with his brothers, he did not exact revenge or even show anger toward them for their mistreatment of him. Instead, he encouraged them not to be distressed over their past actions any longer. Joseph recognized God's hand in his circumstances, and instead of resenting his brothers, he understood and celebrated the way God had accomplished his purpose (Gen 45:4-8). After the death of their father, Joseph again comforted his brothers, telling them that while they had meant him harm, God had used it for good (Gen 50:19-21).

Throughout the stories of the patriarchs, God takes an active and present role. He repeatedly appears to and converses with Abraham (Gen 12:1-3; 15:1-31; 17:1-21; 18:22-33; 22:1-2), Isaac (Gen 26:23-24), and Jacob (Gen 28:12-16; 32:24-30; 35:1, 9-13). God makes them direct promises and tells them exactly what he is going to do. But God never speaks directly to Joseph. Instead, he works in the background of Joseph's story.

Joseph has two dreams that portray his family bowing to him, but God does not explicitly promise Joseph a bright future.

God's purpose is revealed in the eventual fulfillment of Joseph's dreams, but Joseph first has to endure slavery and imprisonment in a foreign land. He suffers the rejection of his brothers, who callously disposed of him because of their jealousy. He suffers through false accusations brought by a woman angered that Joseph rebuffed her advances. His suffering continues when the chief cupbearer forgets him, leaving him to languish in prison for two additional years (Gen 40:23).

While God does not directly speak to Joseph, his hand is evident throughout Joseph's trials. God is with Joseph when he works as a slave in Potiphar's house (Gen 39:2), and he remains with Joseph in prison (Gen 39:21). In all situations, God's presence with Joseph is noticed by others (Gen 39:3, 23), and Joseph gains their favor. It is even noticed by Pharaoh, who promotes Joseph because he recognizes that the spirit of God is in Joseph (Gen 41:38–40).

Joseph's story also illustrates that God fulfills his purpose—sometimes through miraculous and mysterious ways. No matter the circumstances of our life, we can take comfort in knowing that the God of the universe is sovereignly working to accomplish his plan. As Walter Brueggemann writes in his commentary, "The ways of this God are inscrutable. But they are nonetheless sure and reliable. That is something Joseph and his brothers learned only late. But it is foundational for faith."[1] We may not understand God's purpose, but let us—like Joseph—faithfully trust that God will work all things together for good (Rom 8:28).

NOTES

Chapter 1

1. John H. Walton, *Genesis*, The NIV Application Commentary (Grand Rapids, Mich.: Zondervan, 2001), 665.
2. Nahum M. Sarna, *Genesis*, The JPS Torah Commentary (Philadelphia: Jewish Publication Society, 1989), 261.
3. Gordon J. Wenham, *Genesis 16–50*, Word Biblical Commentary, vol. 2 (Dallas: Word, Incorporated, 1998), 356.
4. John H. Walton, *Zondervan Illustrated Bible Backgrounds Commentary (Old Testament) Volume 1: Genesis, Exodus, Leviticus, Numbers, Deuteronomy* (Grand Rapids, Mich.: Zondervan, 2009), 120.
5. Walter A. Elwell, ed., *Baker Encyclopedia of the Bible* (Grand Rapids, Mich.: Baker Book House, 1988), 2110.
6. Mark Sheridan, *Genesis 12–50*. Ancient Christian Commentary on Scripture. Old Testament 2 (Downers Grove, Ill.: InterVarsity Press, 2002), 233–34.
7. Ibid., 235.
8. Ibid., 237–238.

Chapter 2

1. See Edward F. Wente, *Letters from Ancient Egypt*, Writings from the Ancient World, vol. 1 (Atlanta, Ga.: Scholars Press, 1990).
2. The first occurs when his brothers used his robe to convince Jacob of Joseph's death in Genesis 37:31–33.
3. Walton, *Genesis*, 671–72.
4. The terms "forbidden woman" and "adulteress" are used synonymously in Proverbs.
5. For example, Proverbs 3:1–4 ascribes "length of days" and "favor" to those who keep the commands of the book. Other verses show that the wise and righteous will enjoy wealth (Prov 8:18; 14:24).
6. James B. Pritchard, ed., *Ancient Near Eastern Texts Relating to the Old Testament*, 3rd ed. with Supplement (Princeton: Princeton University Press, 1969), 23.

7. William W. Hallo and K. Lawson Younger, eds., *The Context of Scripture*, vol. 1 (Leiden; New York: Brill, 1997), 85.
8. Ibid.
9. Ibid., 86.
10. Ibid.

Chapter 3

1. Wenham, 381.
2. K. A. Kitchen, "Cupbearer," in *New Bible Dictionary*, ed. D. R. W. Wood and I. Howard Marshall (Leicester, England; Downers Grove, Ill.: InterVarsity Press, 1996), 248.
3. Walton, *Zondervan Illustrated Bible Backgrounds Commentary (Old Testament) Volume 1: Genesis, Exodus, Leviticus, Numbers, Deuteronomy*, 127.
4. Hallo and Younger, 77.
5. Ibid., 79.
6. Ideas in this section taken from Kenton L. Sparks, *Ancient Texts for the Study of the Hebrew Bible: A Guide to the Background Literature* (Peabody, Mass.: Hendrickson, 2005), 255.

Chapter 4

1. See "The Interpretation of Dreams," in Pritchard, 495.
2. Walton, *Genesis*, 674.
3. Pritchard, 76–77.
4. Walton, *Genesis*, 674.
5. Ibid.
6. Bruce K. Waltke and Cathi J. Fredricks, *Genesis: A Commentary* (Grand Rapids, Mich.: Zondervan, 2001), 533–34.
7. Victor P. Hamilton, *The Book of Genesis, Chapters 18–50*, The New International Commentary on the Old Testament (Grand Rapids, Mich.: Eerdmans, 1995), 507.
8. James H. Charlesworth, ed., *The Old Testament Pseudepigrapha, Volume 2* (New York: Doubleday, 1985), 203.
9. Ibid.
10. Ibid., 204.
11. Ibid., 211–212.
12. Ibid., 214.
13. Ibid., 220.

Chapter 5

1. Walton, *Zondervan Illustrated Bible Backgrounds Commentary (Old Testament) Volume 1: Genesis, Exodus, Leviticus, Numbers, Deuteronomy*, 132.
2. Refers to Semitic people from Canaan.
3. Hallo and Younger, 108.
4. Ibid., 64.
5. Walton, *Genesis*, 678.

6. Ironically, Job experienced suffering because he was righteous (Job 1:8–11; 2:3–5)—a point that negates his friends' argument.
7. Hallo and Younger, 131.
8. Information in this paragraph from Hallo and Younger, 130.
9. Sparks, 297.

Chapter 6

1. A different use of arrows for divination is seen in Elisha's encounter with the king of Israel, Joash, in 2 Kings 13:14-19.
2. The ancient Babylonians created models of livers with markings to help explain the practice.
3. Joseph and Benjamin were Jacob's only sons through his favorite wife, Rachel (see "Setting the Stage," Chapter 1).
4. See "Setting the Stage," Chapter 5.
5. Hamilton, 570.
6. Thomas C. Oden, ed., "Introduction and Biographical Information," *Ancient Christian Commentary on Scripture* (Downers Grove, Ill.: InterVarsity Press, 1998-2010), 491.
7. Saint Ephraem Syrus, *St. Ephrem the Syrian: Selected Prose Works*, ed. Kathleen E. McVey, trans. Edward G. Mathews and Joseph P. Amar, The Fathers of the Church Vol. 91 (Washington, D.C: Catholic University of America Press, 1994), 192.
8. Ibid., 194.
9. Ibid., 195.

Chapter 7

1. Joseph was 17 when his brothers sold him as a slave (Gen 37:2), and 30 when Pharaoh appointed him over his house (Gen 41:46). Since then there had been seven years of plentiful harvest and two years of famine—a total of 22 years.
2. K. A. Mathews, *Genesis 11:27-50:26*, The New American Commentary, vol. 1B (Nashville: Broadman & Holman Publishers, 2005), 843.
3. Wenham, 445.
4. Hamilton, 604.
5. Sarna, 312.
6. J. H. Charlesworth, *The Old Testament Pseudepigrapha: Volume 1* (New York; London: Yale University Press, 1983), 819.
7. Ibid., 823.

Chapter 8

1. K. A. Kitchen, "Egypt," in *The Zondervan Encyclopedia of the Bible* (Grand Rapids, Mich.: Zondervan, 2009), 279.
2. Michael O. Wise, Martin G. Abegg, Jr., and Edward M. Cook, *The Dead Sea Scrolls: A New Translation* (San Francisco: HarperSanFrancisco, 2005), 355. The square brackets in this scroll fragment indicate missing or reconstructed words.

Conclusion

1. Walter Brueggemann, *Genesis*, Interpretation: A Bible Commentary for Teaching and Preaching (Atlanta, GA: John Knox Press, 1982), 294.

SOURCES

Alexander, T. Desmond, and David W. Baker, eds. *Dictionary of the Old Testament: Pentateuch.* Downers Grove, Ill.: InterVarsity Press, 2003.

Begg, Alistair. *The Hand of God: Finding His Care in All Circumstances.* Chicago, Ill.: Moody, 1999.

Blenkinsopp, Joseph. *The Pentateuch: An Introduction to the First Five Books of the Bible.* New Haven: Yale University Press, 1992.

Bromiley, Geoffrey W., ed. *The International Standard Bible Encyclopedia, Revised.* 4 vols. Grand Rapids, Mich.: Eerdmans, 1988.

Brueggemann, Walter. *Genesis.* Interpretation. Atlanta, Ga.: John Knox, 1982.

Charlesworth, James H., ed. *The Old Testament Pseudepigrapha.* 2 vols. New York: Doubleday, 1983-1985.

Coats, John R. *Original Sinners: A New Interpretation of Genesis.* New York: Free Press, 2009.

Elwell, Walter A., ed. *Baker Encyclopedia of the Bible.* Grand Rapids, Mich.: Baker, 1988.

Ephraem, Syrus, Saint. *St. Ephrem the Syrian: Selected Prose Works.* Edited by Kathleen E. McVey. Translated by Edward G. Mathews and Joseph P. Amar. The Fathers of the Church vol. 91. Washington, D.C: Catholic University of America Press, 1994.

Gruen, Erich S. *Heritage and Hellenism: The Reinvention of Jewish Tradition.* Berkeley, Calif.: University of California Press, 2002.

Hallo, William W., and K. Lawson Younger Jr., eds. *The Context of Scripture, Volume I: Canonical Compositions from the Biblical World.* Leiden: Brill, 1997.

Hamilton, Victor P. *The Book of Genesis, Chapters 18-50.* The New International Commentary on the Old Testament. Grand Rapids, Mich.: Eerdmans, 1995.

Hoffmeier, James Karl. *Israel in Egypt: The Evidence for the Authenticity of the Exodus Tradition.* New York: Oxford University Press, 1999.

Kugel, James L. *In Potiphar's House: The Interpretive Life of Biblical Texts.* Cambridge, Mass.: Harvard University Press, 1994.

Mathews, K. A. *Genesis 11:27–50:26.* Vol. 1B. The New American Commentary. Nashville: Broadman & Holman, 2005.

Oden, Thomas C., ed. *Ancient Christian Commentary on Scripture.* 28 vols. Downers Grove, Ill.: Inter-Varsity Press, 1998.

Pritchard, James B., ed. *Ancient Near Eastern Texts Relating to the Old Testament.* 3rd ed. with Supplement. Princeton: Princeton University Press, 1969.

Sarna, Nahum M. *Genesis.* The JPS Torah Commentary. Philadelphia: The Jewish Publication Society, 1989.

Sparks, Kenton L. *Ancient Texts for the Study of the Hebrew Bible: A Guide to the Background Literature.* Peabody, Mass.: Hendrickson Publishers, 2005.

Tenney, Merrill C., and Moisés Silva, eds. *The Zondervan Encyclopedia of the Bible.* 5 vols. Revised, Full-Color Edition. Grand Rapids, Mich.: Zondervan, 2009.

VanderKam, James C. *The Dead Sea Scrolls Today.* Grand Rapids, Mich.: Eerdmans, 1994.

Waltke, Bruce K., and Cathi J. Fredricks. *Genesis: a Commentary.* Grand Rapids, Mich.: Zondervan, 2001.

Walton, John H. *Zondervan Illustrated Bible Backgrounds Commentary (Old Testament) Volume 1: Genesis, Exodus, Leviticus, Numbers, Deuteronomy.* Grand Rapids, Mich.: Zondervan, 2009.

Walton, John H. *Genesis.* The NIV Application Commentary. Grand Rapids, Mich.: Zondervan, 2001.

Water, Mark. *The Book of Genesis Made Easy.* Alresford, Hampshire: John Hunt Publishers Ltd, 2000.

Wenham, Gordon J. *Genesis 16–50.* Word Biblical Commentary, vol. 2. Dallas, Tex.: Word, 1998.

Wente, Edward F. *Letters from Ancient Egypt.* Edited by Edmund S. Meltzer. Writings from the Ancient World 1. Atlanta, Ga.: Scholars Press, 1990.

White, Jerry E. *The Joseph Road: Choices That Determine Your Destiny.* Colorado Springs, Colo.: NavPress, 2009.

Wilcox, Pete. *Living the Dream: Joseph for Today: A Dramatic Exposition of Genesis 37–50.* Milton Keynes, UK: Paternoster, 2007.

Wilson, Lindsay. *Joseph, Wise and Otherwise: The Intersection of Wisdom and Covenant in Genesis 37-50*. Milton Keynes, UK: Paternoster, 2004.

Wise, Michael Owen, Martin G. Abegg, and Edward M. Cook. *The Dead Sea Scrolls: A New Translation*. Rev. ed. San Francisco: HarperSanFrancisco, 2005.

Wood, D. R. W., I. Howard Marshall, A. R. Millard, J. I. Packer, and D. J. Wiseman, eds. *New Bible Dictionary*. 3rd ed. Leicester, England; Downers Grove, IL: Inter-Varsity Press; InterVarsity Press, 1996.

ABOUT THE EDITOR

Michael R. Grigoni has served as managing editor of Bible reference for Lexham Press. He holds a Master of Theological Studies from Harvard Divinity School and an MA in music from the University of Washington.

ABOUT THE AUTHORS

Derek R. Brown is a contributing editor for the Lexham Bible Guides: Paul's Letters Collection. He holds a PhD in New Testament Studies and Christian Origins from the University of Edinburgh and a Masters of Arts in New Testament Studies from Regent College.

Miles Custis is the author of *The End of the Matter: Understanding the Epilogue of Ecclesiastes*, a Faithlife Study Bible contributing editor, the co-author of Lexham Bible Guides: Genesis Collection, and the coauthor of *Jacob: Discerning God's Presence* and three other Studies in Faithful Living volumes. In addition, he is a regular *Bible Study Magazine* and *Lexham Bible Dictionary* contributor. He holds a Master of Arts in biblical studies from Trinity Western University.

Douglas Mangum is the editor of the Lexham Bible Guides series and the Lexham Methods Series, the coauthor of Lexham Bible Guides: Genesis Collection, and the coauthor of *Mary: Devoted to God's Plan* and three other Studies in Faithful Living volumes. He is a Lexham English Bible editor, a Faithlife Study Bible contributing editor, a regular *Bible Study Magazine* contributor, and a frequently consulted specialist for the *Lexham Bible Dictionary*. In addition, he is a PhD candidate in Near Eastern studies at the University of Free State; he holds a Master of Arts in Hebrew and Semitic studies from the University of Wisconsin–Madison.

Matthew M. Whitehead is the coauthor of *Lexham Bible Guide: Ephesians* and three Studies in Faithful Living volumes. He has also served as a Faithlife Study Bible contributing editor and *Bible Study Magazine* contributor. He assisted with the digitization process for the Discoveries in the Judaean Desert series and worked on the Oxford Hebrew Bible project. Matthew holds an MDiv from Northwest Baptist Seminary and is pursuing an MA in biblical studies at Trinity Western University.

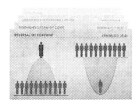

Discover More with Lexham Press

Lexham Press advances scholarship and equips the church. We are an imprint of Faithlife Corporation, makers of Logos Bible Software. As such, our ideas are built on over 20 years of experience serving the church. Visit **LexhamPress.com** to learn more.

Each volume in the Not Your Average Bible Study series guides you step-by-step through Scripture, helping you discover powerful insights as you move through the text, digging into the Bible on a whole new level. With discussion and reflection questions, specific prayer suggestions, and ideas for further study, you'll see how easy it is to apply these lessons to your everyday life.

Much of what we learn serves an immediate purpose, but God's Word has eternal value. That's why it is vital that we seek His Spirit daily through prayer and Bible study. Connect the Testaments is a 365-day devotional with a custom reading plan that covers the entire Bible over one year, explaining difficult and complex passages along the way.

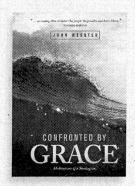

This rich collection of thoughtful sermons from one of the leading contemporary theologians is challenging, stimulating, and inspiring. These reflections, born from years of theological and biblical study, demonstrate the complexity of the realities we face in the Christian life and the depth of the grace of God.

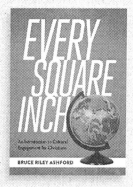

Drawing on such sources as Abraham Kuyper, Francis Schaeffer, and C.S. Lewis, Bruce Ashford argues that God wants our whole lives to be shaped by Jesus' lordship. If Jesus truly is Lord over everything, then our faith is relevant to every dimension of culture.